MILLIONS OF MILES TO MARS

A JOURNEY TO THE RED PLANET

BY JOSEPH W. KELCH
ILLUSTRATIONS BY CONNELL PATRICK BYRNE

Julian Ⓜ Messner
Published by Silver Burdett Press
Parsippany, New Jersey

PHOTO ACKNOWLEDGMENTS:

Department of the Interior, U.S. Geological Survey: pages 120–121.

The Lowell Observatory, Flagstaff, Arizona: pages 13 and 14. Used by permission.

Movie Stills Archive: page 15.

NASA: pages 18, 19, 20, 22–23, 30, 31, 58, 59, 69, 70–71, 72, 73, 74, 75, 76–77, 82, 83, 100, 104.

Leroy Williams—courtesy of Maryland Science Center, Baltimore, Maryland: pages 10 and 12.

To Ian and Amanda

JULIAN MESSNER
Published by Silver Burdett Press
250 James Street
Morristown, NJ 07960
Copyright ©1995 by Joseph W. Kelch
All rights reserved including the right of reproduction in whole or in part in any form.

JULIAN MESSNER and colophon are trademarks of Simon & Schuster.
Designed by Virginia Pope
Manufactured in the United States of America
10 9 8 7 6 5 4 3 2 1

Library of Congress Cataloging-in-Publication Data
Kelch, Joseph W.
Millions of Miles to Mars by Joseph William Kelch; illustrations by Connell Patrick Byrne.
      p. cm.
      Includes index
1. Mars (Planet)—Exploration—Juvenile literature. 2. Space flight to Mars—
      Juvenile literature. [1. Mars (Planet)—Exploration. 2. Space flight to Mars.]
      I. Byrne, Connell, ill. II. Title.
QB641.K3 1995
919.9'2304—dc20 93-33798 CIP AC
ISBN: 0-671-88249-X

CONTENTS

WHY MARS?

The spacecraft seat you are sitting in is very comfortable. Normally you might even find yourself tempted to take a nap. But not today! You are about to begin a great journey. You have been in Earth's orbit for about three weeks. During that time you have been kept under close watch, to be sure you are not carrying any diseases, even the common cold.

You were assigned a cabin on board the space station but spent much of your time aboard the large spacecraft docked to the station. It will be your home for much of the next two years. You have a nice cabin on this spacecraft too and have decorated it with things that will remind you of your friends and family on Earth.

You spent only a little time with other members of the crew. Since you will see a lot of them during the mission, you tried to see and talk with other people on the station. It will be a long time before you have a chance to make any new friends.

This morning you said good-bye to the station crew and climbed aboard the docked spacecraft. The commander of the mission spoke to the crew about what fortunate people you are to be the first to make this journey. You are too excited to think much about that.

About an hour ago you pulled on your flight suit and got ready for the launch. Up on the flight deck of the *spaceship are seats for each one of the eight members of the crew. Only the commander and pilot have seats in front, where the cockpit windows give a beautiful view of the space station.*

The spacecraft finally undocks from the station. Small thruster engines fire to move it slowly away. The station begins to shrink, drifting farther and farther away. Other thrusters fire. The spacecraft begins to turn, aiming itself along a new path. A few moments later all is quiet. Seemingly floating motionless, in fact the spacecraft is traveling around Earth at over 17,000 miles (27,370 km) per hour.

A low rumble shakes the spacecraft. The mighty nuclear engines have begun to fire. Now you will leave the orbit of Earth, heading into deep space. Awaiting you, some six months from now, is the red planet Mars.

When I was a child, I had a book called *You Will Go to the Moon.* I believed it! There was no question in my mind that one day I would be bouncing around the Moon's surface just like the Apollo astronauts I saw on TV. This was very exciting. I could hardly wait to grow up.

I knew that to go to the Moon I would have to study science and math very hard. Even though my teachers never taught even one day of astronomy, I took out every book on space I could find from the school and public libraries.

Sadly, many people have decided that space travel is not as important as other things here on Earth. As I grew older, I realized that my chances of going to the Moon any time soon were very unlikely. I still loved space though and decided to find a way to help others who wanted to learn about astronomy. That is why I work in a **planetarium**, a place where all kinds of people, young and old, come to learn about space. I still hope that some day I will get to go to the Moon or, even better, the planet Mars!

Would you like to go to Mars? What is Mars and where is it located? Has anyone been there? How long does it take to get there? Is there life on Mars? The following pages will provide some answers to these questions.

Earth is our home planet. It travels around the Sun on a path called an orbit. The orbit of Earth looks like a circle but actually it is not perfectly round. On average, Earth is about 92,900,000 miles (149,500,000 km) from the Sun. In January Earth is only about 91,500,000 miles (147,300,000 km) from the Sun, but in July it is about 94,500,000 miles (152,150,000 km) from the Sun. The shape of the orbit of Earth is called an **ellipse**, or oval. An egg has a shape that is kind of like an ellipse. So does a football.

Earth is not the only planet that orbits the Sun. We know of nine planets altogether. Two of them are closer to the Sun than Earth. They are called Mercury and Venus. Six others are farther from the Sun than Earth. They are Mars, Jupiter, Saturn, Uranus, Neptune, and Pluto. All

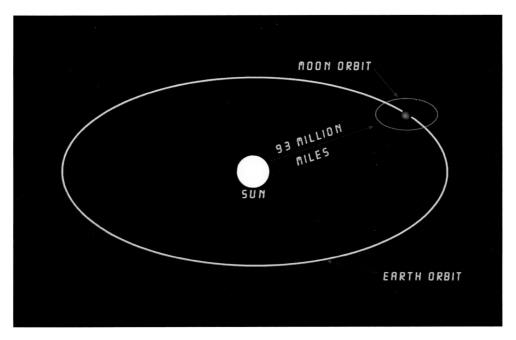

The Moon orbits Earth while Earth orbits the Sun.

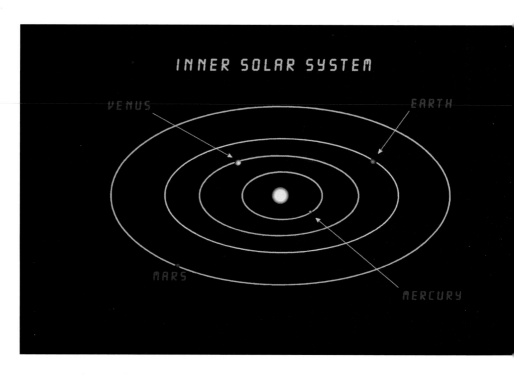

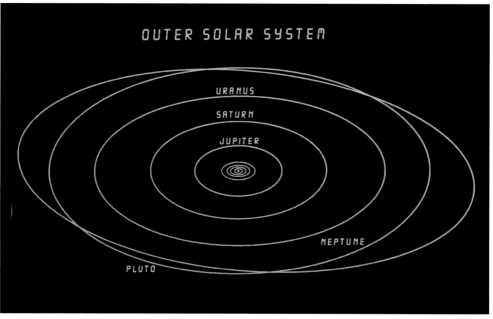

Top: The planets of the inner solar system. Bottom: The planets of the outer solar system.

Worlds of the Solar System

Stars:	One (The Sun)	**1**
Planets:	Nine	**9**
Moons:	Sixty	**60**
Asteroids:	Nine Thousand	**9000**
Comets:	Billions	**1,000,000,000+**

There are many different worlds in our solar system. Similar worlds may exist around other stars as well.

these planets travel along orbits around the Sun, just like Earth. The orbits of the other planets are also ellipses. Some of them, like Mercury and Pluto, are much less like circles than Earth's orbit. These planets change their distance from the Sun by quite a bit during each orbit.

We also find other worlds here. There are moons orbiting many of the planets, just like our Moon orbits Earth. Between Mars and Jupiter is a great belt of large rocks called the Asteroid Belt. Far beyond Pluto are billions of chunks of icy rock called comets. All these worlds together are called the **solar system**.

Earth is the third planet out from the Sun. Mars is the fourth. That means Mars is one of our closest neighbors in the solar system. No wonder it has long been one of the most talked about and studied of the planets!

Have you looked at the night sky? How many stars did you see? Too many to count! Did you know that not all those little points of light are stars? Some are planets. Mars is one of the planets we can look for in the sky. How do you tell a planet from a star? No, you don't need a telescope to tell the difference.

Stars are so far away that they appear as only tiny points of light no matter how powerful a telescope you use. A telescope can allow you to

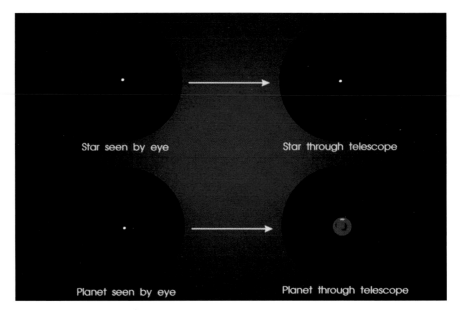

| Star seen by eye | Star through telescope |
| Planet seen by eye | Planet through telescope |

Stars are so far away that even powerful telescopes are unable to show a disk. Planet disks can be seen with even small telescopes.

see a planet as a disk. However, people were able to identify planets in the sky thousands of years before the invention of the telescope. There must be other ways to tell the difference.

Have you ever noticed that stars sometimes seem to twinkle? This happens because the light from the star has to travel through the atmosphere of our planet before reaching our eyes. The atmosphere is not very steady. Winds are always blowing around high above our heads. The air is filled with particles of dust. Some of the dust comes from natural occurrences like volcanoes. Other dust comes from our factory smokestacks. Light from stars is traveling in a straight line as it enters the atmosphere. When it encounters dust, some of the light is reflected off the dust. This allows less light to make it through to us. Very briefly, the light from the star is dimmed. Since the star is visible as only a tiny point of light, even a small dust particle can block out most of the light from the star. On hot days you may see heat rising from a road. The air seems to shimmer. Heat rising in our atmosphere does the same thing to starlight. This adds to the twinkling effect of stars.

Planets are not just points of light. They are really small disks as seen from Earth. Dust particles are usually not big enough to block out most of the light from a planet. Planet light is not dimmed as much by dust. Heat in the atmosphere will not cause the larger image of a planet to shimmer as much either.

On the next clear night, look at the stars. Are they twinkling? Then look around carefully, especially at the brighter stars. Do any of them *not* twinkle like the others? These may be planets. One of them may even be Mars!

Long ago people watched the sky more often and carefully. They noticed occurrences happening over long periods of time. The stars they saw formed patterns that slowly drifted across the sky as the seasons passed. Each year the same groups of stars were seen. These patterns, the constellations, remained the same. They were called **fixed stars**.

Five other stars were seen to be moving among the constellations. These were named planets, a term that means wandering star. These five planets didn't go speeding across the sky in a single night. It took weeks or even months for a planet to move from one constellation into the next.

If you watch the sky carefully for several weeks, perhaps you can find a star that moves among the other stars. It is not easy if you don't know the sky very well. If you want to find a planet, you can probably call your local planetarium or even the newspaper and someone there can tell you where to look. Ask them where to find Mars. It may not

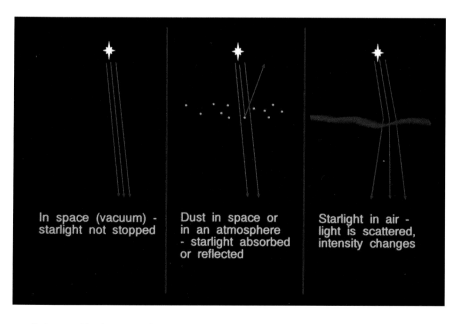

In space (vacuum) - starlight not stopped

Dust in space or in an atmosphere - starlight absorbed or reflected

Starlight in air - light is scattered, intensity changes

Starlight twinkles because of the effects of atmosphere and dust.

be in the sky when you ask. Sometimes Mars is on the far side of the Sun from here on Earth. That means Mars would be in the daytime sky right near the Sun and would be very hard to see. If you are lucky, Mars will be in the evening sky.

The people of long ago who watched Mars noticed another very strange thing about its motion in the sky. Every two years, when Mars appeared brightest, it would move in the pattern of a loop in the sky. Mars appeared bright at this time because it was closer to Earth than usual. Mars travels slower than Earth in its orbit, so Earth catches up and passes Mars as the two planets circle the Sun. Earth passes Mars once every 780 days, a little more than two years. As Earth passes it, Mars seems to move backward against the background of stars. This motion, called a **retrograde loop**, happens to all planets more distant from the Sun than Earth. It is most obvious, however, with Mars.

Now that we know how to find Mars in the sky, let's find out something about what Mars is like. When did we learn the things we know about Mars?

The average distance between the Sun and Mars is 141,000,000 miles (227,010,000 km). It takes 687 days, nearly two years, for Mars to complete one orbit of the Sun. It is about 4,200 miles (6,762 km) across, just over half the size of Earth. This might make it seem a small planet, but since Mars does not have any oceans the amount of land surface is actually very similar to Earth's. Mars rotates, or spins around, its axis once every 24 hours and 37 minutes. This is very close to the rotation time of Earth, so Mars has a day and night cycle very similar to ours. Mars has two small moons, Phobos and Deimos.

Early telescopes showed very little of what the Martian surface was like, visible only as a reddish or orange object in the night sky. The orange color was there along with some darker, almost greenish, patches and brighter polar caps. Since the planet was rather small, it didn't appear very large even when viewed through the most powerful early telescopes.

In 1877 Mars was approaching **opposition**, when it is closest to Earth. Many astronomers prepared to observe Mars, using some of the best telescopes of that time. One of these astronomers was Giovanni

Earth		Mars	
3rd planet		4th planet	
Diameter:	7980 miles	Diameter:	4200 miles
Rotation period:	23 hr 56 min	Rotation period:	24 hr 37 min
Orbital period:	365.25 days	Orbital period:	687 days
Distance from Sun:	92.9 million miles	Distance from Sun:	141 million miles
Gravity:	32 feet/sec^2	Gravity:	12 feet/sec^2
Atmosphere:	Nitrogen/Oxygen	Atmosphere:	Carbon Dioxide
Temperature Day:	68°F (20°C)	Temperature Day:	-20°F (-43°C)
Temperature Night:	50°F (10°C)	Temperature Night:	-120°F (-99°C)

Comparison of Earth and Mars.

Schiaparelli (pronounced ski-ap-a-relly), an Italian. He had a good telescope and was well known for his excellent observations. He set to work watching Mars and drawing pictures of what he saw. His pictures were so important in creating an image of what Mars was like that people would talk about them for the next one hundred years.

Schiaparelli drew Mars with many features that appeared to be straight lines. He labeled these *canali*, an Italian word that means channels. To Schiaparelli, these were most likely natural features formed by water or cracks in the surface as a result of great Marsquakes.

Outside Italy, the word canali caused great excitement. At that time work was under way on the Suez Canal in Egypt that would connect the Mediterranean and Red Seas. One of the world's great engineering feats, the Suez Canal represented the greatest intelligence and accomplishments of humans.

Canali was mistranslated as canals by many who assumed that Mars was the home of another intelligent, accomplished, technical race of beings. Apparently more than one great canal existed on Mars, but indeed the planet appeared to be covered with these artificial waterways. Martians then might actually be more advanced than humans!

At the same time Giovanni Schiaparelli was examining the canali, another astronomer, Asaph Hall, was hard at work at the U.S. Naval Observatory in Washington, D.C. He was searching for moons of

Giovanni Schiaparelli directed the observatory in Milan, Italy.

Mars, using the most powerful telescope of the time, a 26-inch (66-cm) **refractor**.

Astronomers previously had identified moons around five of the known planets. (Pluto was unknown since it was not discovered until 1930.) Mercury and Venus had no moons. Earth of course had one. Jupiter had the four discovered by Galileo (12 other moons were still to be discovered). Saturn had nine (12 moons still unknown). Four (out of 15) were known about Uranus and one (out of eight) around Neptune.

Scientists of the time often looked for logical mathematical progressions in nature. When examining the pattern of known moons in the solar system, they saw what appeared to be a doubling of moons out to Saturn and then cutting the number in half for each planet after Saturn. Only Mars and the recently discovered (in 1846) Neptune strayed from this pattern. Many expected to find another moon of

Neptune. That left just Mars. According to the pattern, there should have been two moons around Mars. Hall was determined to find them.

As the summer of 1877 progressed with no luck, Hall began to tire of the search. If there were moons of Mars, they would have to be much smaller than the moons of other planets or they would have been found easily. Hall's wife, Angeline, told Asaph not to give up. He continued his search, and on August 11 and 16 he observed a small dot near Mars that was indeed a moon. He discovered another, even closer to Mars, on August 17. They were very faint and most likely very small.

Hall decided to name the two moons Phobos and Deimos, after attendants of Mars, the ancient god of war. Phobos, the inner moon, means fear in Greek. Deimos, the outer moon, means panic or terror.

Soon Mars became an interesting subject of discussion not only among astronomers but also among the general public. People were fascinated by the possibility of life on a world so close to ours. Many observers continued to hunt for the canali of Schiaparelli. The canali proved difficult to see under most conditions as were the tiny moons, usually hidden within the glare of Mars itself.

In 1892 Schiaparelli announced his retirement from astronomical observation. One of his admirers, a Boston banker named Percival Lowell, decided to continue his work. Though not a trained

Moons of the Solar System - 1875

	Known	Expected
Mercury-	0	0
Venus-	0	0
Earth-	1	1
Mars-	0	2
Jupiter-	4	4
Saturn-	8	8
Uranus-	4	4
Neptune-	1	2

In the past scientists often looked for neat mathematical patterns in nature. They thought such a pattern might exist in the number of moons in the solar system.

Above: Percival Lowell came from a wealthy Boston family. He spent many years travel-ing throughout the world. During one of his trips he became obsessed with Mars and devoted the rest of his life to studying the red planet. Right: Percival Lowell at work in his observatory in Arizona.

astronomer, he had learned a great deal about astronomy in his free time. He decided to build his own observatory in Flagstaff, Arizona, where clear, dry skies allowed for excellent viewing. Lowell and his observatory soon became famous. He spent long hours looking at Mars through his big telescope. He drew pictures of what he saw and made globes of Mars based on his drawings.

Lowell's drawings and globes of Mars included many crisscrossing lines. At the intersections of these lines were dark spots. Lowell believed the lines were canals bringing water to the Martian cities. The cities were the dark spots. He imagined a very ancient race of Martians living on a mostly dry planet. The canals brought water from the polar ice caps, which could also be seen with good telescopes. People were very excited by Lowell's observations.

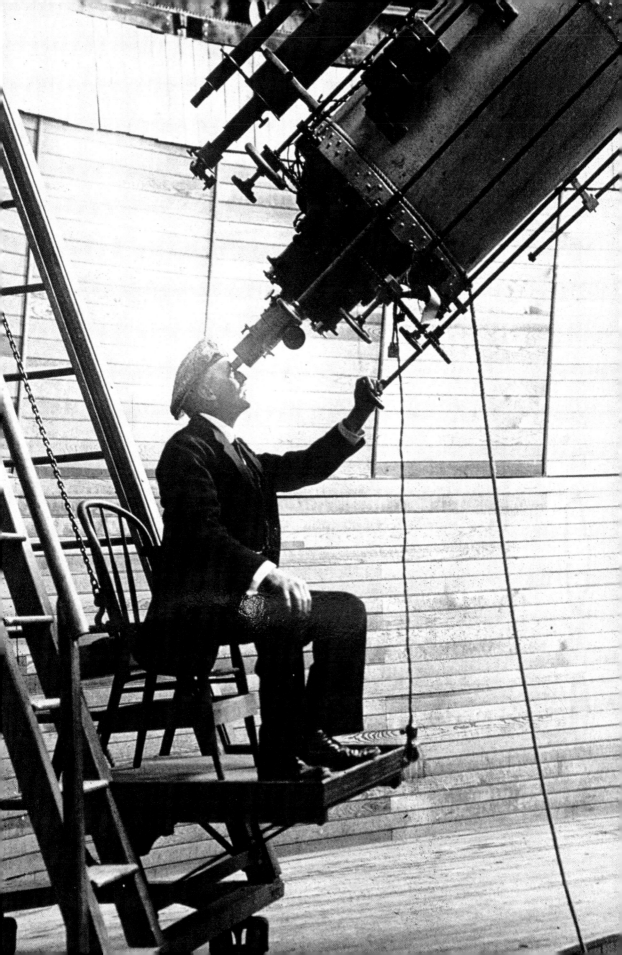

In 1898 a book appeared called *The War of the Worlds*. Written by H.G. Wells, and based on the theories of Lowell, this book described an invasion of Earth by Martians. The Martians had become tired of their dry world and had come to Earth for the plentiful supply of

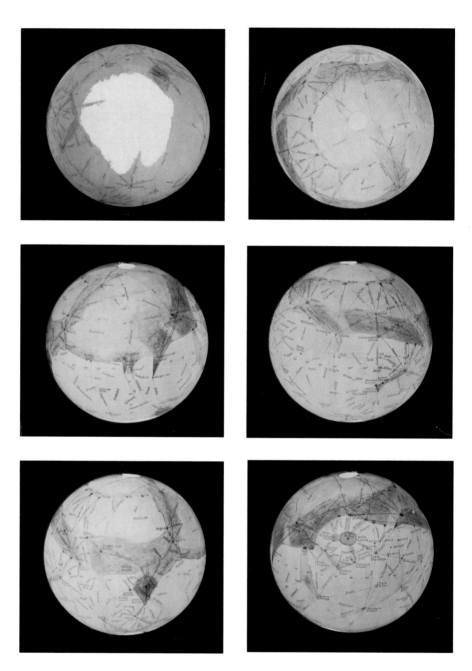

Six views of Percival Lowell's globe of Mars. Canals are clearly visible. The dark spots where canals meet were thought to be cities.

In 1953 Hollywood produced a full-color, special-effects-filled version of the H. G. Wells classic, The War of the Worlds. *The film's vivid images of Martian war machines frightened a generation of moviegoers.*

water. Unfortunately, they were unwilling to share it with the human beings already living here. A fierce battle began, and only the smallest of earthly life-forms could save the day.

Other authors were enchanted by the thought of life on Mars. Edgar Rice Burroughs, creator of Tarzan, wrote a series of books about a Martian civilization called "Barsoom." Though also fierce fighters, Burroughs' Martians did not yet travel to other planets.

Throughout the first half of the twentieth century, scientists continued to observe Mars through telescopes. Some saw the canali, some did not. They also began to wonder if Mars would have the right conditions for life.

Life exists on Earth partly because our planet is the right distance from the Sun to get enough light and heat. Too close to the Sun and it would be too hot. Too far away and it would be frigid winter at all times. In between is a region called the **Life Zone**.

Was Mars within the Life Zone? Astronomers were not sure. Some believed the Life Zone was wide enough for both Venus and Mars. Others thought it was much narrower. Many things can help make a planet warm or cold. The atmosphere of a planet acts like a blanket to hold in heat. Some gases, such as water vapor and carbon dioxide, are very good at holding in heat. Other gases, like nitrogen, allow heat to escape easily. Was the atmosphere of Mars thick enough and made of the right gases for the planet to be warm and for life to exist?

Water is also very important to life on Earth. Scientists wondered how much water would be found on Mars. The reddish color of the planet indicated it was mostly desert. There was no sign of great oceans. The polar caps probably contained some water. However, these polar caps seemed to shrink quite a bit during the summer months, more than the polar caps of Earth. This might mean the caps were very thin and melted easily. There might not be very much water on Mars.

Since Mars is farther from the Sun than Earth, it travels more slowly in its orbit. This means that each season on Mars is longer than on Earth. A long summer might allow more of the polar cap to melt. Maybe there was a lot of water in the polar caps of Mars, but they had a long time in which to melt.

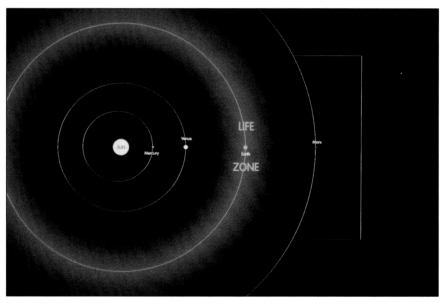

Our planet orbits within a Life Zone, where light and heat from the Sun are just right to support life.

To determine temperature and water conditions, scientists needed to get a closer look at Mars than they could get through telescopes. That chance finally arrived in the 1960s when the **Space Age** began.

In 1964 the space probe *Mariner 4* was launched toward Mars. *Mariner 4* was not very advanced, but it did include a simple camera capable of sending back a few pictures to Earth as it flew past Mars in 1965. Twenty-two pictures in all were returned. The photos showed a world very different from what many expected.

A world of canals was not what *Mariner 4* showed us. Instead the fuzzy pictures were filled with craters, most looking just like the ones found on the Moon. No sign indicated that rain or wind had worn away these craters, so there probably wasn't much air or water on Mars. It was a big disappointment to those hoping to find life on Mars.

Other spacecraft came to Mars, although now the excitement of exploring the planet was not as great. *Mariner 6* and *Mariner 7* in 1969 found more craters and got the first look at the southern polar cap of Mars. This polar cap turned out to be made up mostly of dry ice, frozen carbon dioxide. Now it seemed that there was probably not much water on Mars at all! The temperature on Mars was extremely cold, reaching to more than 100° Fahrenheit below zero (-73° Celsius), even at the equator. The red planet was a dry, cold desert where no life could exist.

Then in 1971 a more advanced spacecraft, *Mariner 9*, was sent to Mars. Instead of a brief flyby of the planet, *Mariner 9* was designed to orbit Mars. This would allow more pictures and other experiments. Most people paid little attention to this mission since Mars no longer seemed as interesting a planet. Quietly, the scientists waited as the little spacecraft approached the planet.

No other spacecraft had ever attempted to orbit another planet. *Mariner 9* was the first, and on November 13, 1971, it succeeded. Scientists got ready to start learning more about Mars.

Unfortunately, at the time of *Mariner 9*'s arrival there was a great dust storm on Mars. In fact, the entire planet was covered by thick clouds of dust that completely hid the surface from view. Photographing the planet had to wait several months for the dust to clear. In the meantime *Mariner 9* told scientists a lot about weather on Mars. There was also time to take pictures of the Martian moons.

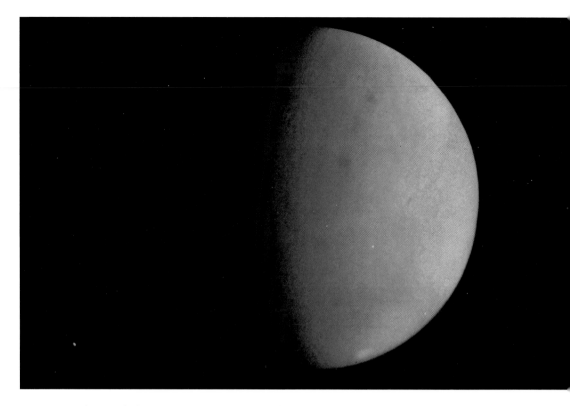

Planetwide dust storm on Mars. Several of the largest volcanoes are just visible as darker spots in the dust.

Finally the storm began to clear. The first thing *Mariner 9* saw was four dark spots protruding from the dust. What looked like craters were seen at the center of these spots. At first these were thought to be simply mountains with impact craters near their tops. As the pictures became clearer, it was seen that these were actually huge volcanoes. This was a very unexpected discovery.

Other features began to appear in the pictures from *Mariner 9*. Sand dunes, blown by the wind, were found scattered about the floors of many craters. Long, thin valleys, looking much like dried riverbeds, could be seen in many places. The northern polar cap turned out to be very different from the southern cap. It contained mostly water ice instead of dry ice. A supply of water did exist on Mars after all, though the atmosphere was too thin to allow water to exist in a liquid form. All water on Mars was either frozen or it quickly boiled away into water vapor, even in the cold temperatures of Mars. Most days the temperatures remained below zero.

One of the most spectacular things found by *Mariner 9* was a huge canyon called Valles Marineris, or the Mariner Valley. Similar to the Grand Canyon on Earth, this canyon is much larger. Valles Marineris stretches a distance equal to that from Los Angeles, California, to New York City! It is about 4 miles (6 km) deep in some places and more than 100 miles (161 km) wide. Some mornings the canyon is filled with clouds, a sign that water can be found in the atmosphere of Mars. This canyon may have been cut by running water long ago.

Suddenly Mars was interesting again. Though certainly not home to any advanced intelligent civilization, there was again the possibility of simple life-forms being found on the planet. Scientists were encouraged as they designed experiments for the next mission to Mars, the Vikings.

Viking 1 and *Viking 2* were launched less than one month apart in the late summer of 1975. Each included two spacecraft, an orbiter, and

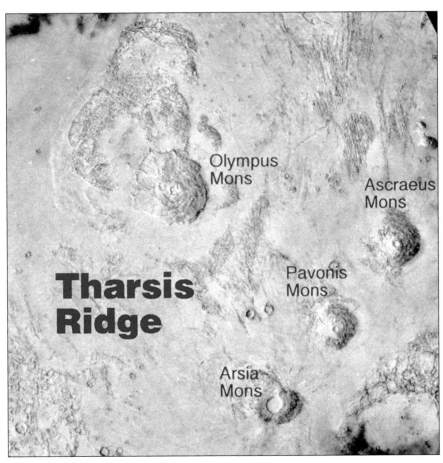

The major volcanoes of Mars as based on Viking data.

Tracks in the Martian surface made by the scoop on a Viking spacecraft. An arm of the spacecraft is in the middle of the picture.

a lander. It was hoped that this mission could answer many of the questions about Mars. *Viking 1* and *Viking 2* arrived at Mars during the summer of 1976. No dust storm this time interfered as the orbiters began taking pictures. The first thing to do was find a good place for the landers to set down. To make the chances of success better, scientists wanted a smooth place where the spacecraft would not be tipped over by rocks or cliffs.

Viking 1 landed in a place called Chryse Planitia, Plain of Gold, on July 20, 1976. This was exactly seven years after the Apollo astronauts first landed on the Moon. Cameras on the lander quickly began operating. The first pictures arrived back on Earth, and the scientists had their first look at the soil of Mars.

These first views included a stretch of dirt with many scattered small rocks. It was a startling image, very crisp and detailed. Soon another image arrived, this one showing the distant horizon and a plain filled with rocks, boulders, and drifts of sand and dust—a desolate, lonely place.

On board the lander, experiments were readied that would look for life. Samples of soil were collected by a small shovel and brought on board the craft. Within a small automatic laboratory, water and food were added to the Martian soil. Sensors looked for signs of life. These might include gases released by breathing organisms or waste products produced by creatures as they fed.

The first result was a shock. A burst of oxygen was produced by adding nutrients to a sample. On Earth this would indicate photosynthesis, a process that occurs in plants where nutrients and carbon dioxide are used to produce energy for the plants and oxygen is released. The scientists were cautious, however. Instead of announcing that they had found life on Mars, they continued to watch the sample. The release of oxygen began to diminish. Thriving life would have continued to produce oxygen. Scientists began to think that there might be some chemical reaction taking place in the soil that produced the first blast of oxygen. Once used up, the reaction slowed and stopped. The other experiments also failed to prove any form of life existed on Mars. The results were not certain, but most scientists today believe there is no life on Mars.

Viking 2 landed in a region known as Utopia Planitia, Plain of Utopia. It performed many of the same experiments and recorded similar results. Still, only two locations on all of Mars have been directly studied. A lot of Mars is still waiting to be seen close up. Two spacecraft landing on Earth would be likely to land either in the ocean or in forest or desert, which would not tell much about human life on our planet. More exploration will be needed to know for certain whether any life exists on Mars.

The Viking orbiters remained in operation for years, taking thousands of detailed pictures of the planet. Maps of Mars have been made from these pictures. With these maps future trips to Mars can be aimed toward the most interesting areas of the planet. Scientists will want to study places near where rivers may have once flowed. The edges of the polar caps may supply enough water for life. Are the volcanoes on Mars still active? Some of these questions can be answered by robotic space probes. Many people, however, feel the best way to do this kind of exploration is with human beings.

Are we ready to go to Mars? Do we know how to do it? How much will it cost? These are just a few of the questions people ask when they discuss a trip to Mars. In this book we will look at some of the things we need to know if we are going to go *Millions of Miles to Mars*!

A picture of the Martian surface as taken by the Viking spacecraft. Will the first humans on Mars see a landscape like this?

PLOTTING A COURSE

For thirty minutes the nuclear engines continue to fire. You can feel the acceleration of the spacecraft pushing you into the cushions of your seat. The most powerful rocket engines in the solar system are propelling you into space.

Suddenly they stop. Silence returns. The commander turns and says with a smile, "We're on our way!"

That means the engines performed well. We are now moving at over 35,000 miles (56,350 km) per hour, faster than any humans in history. We are leaving Earth.

Out of your seat you go, the zero gravity allowing you to float easily into the air. Pushing against walls, ceiling, and floor, you make your way over to a window. Only darkness is visible, with bright stars shining as steady points of light.

Then you see a breathtaking sight. Earth is there, blue and cloud-covered, a pretty world indeed. You will miss it as the many miles pile up between you and the world where you were born. You wonder what it will be like to see it again two years from now.

Somewhere out ahead is a new world, unexplored and full of mystery. That is your next stop!

Getting from place to place here on Earth seems pretty easy. If you have a map, you can easily find out what roads will get you where you want to go. When you play basketball, you know exactly where the ball must go in order to score a basket. When you get hungry, the refrigerator holds just what you need, and it's always easy to find. Traveling in space, though, is a lot more difficult.

Things in space don't usually stay in the same place. They are always in motion. Planets, moons, asteroids, comets, and even stars are all traveling through space at all times. And, in most cases, everything is going in different directions. It doesn't do you much good to look out and see where something is right now and just head in that direction. By the time you get there, it will have moved. It might be millions of miles away!

Getting somewhere in space takes a lot of planning. You must know exactly how everything is moving. Take a football outside with a friend. If you both stand still and throw the ball back and forth, it's pretty easy to get the ball to each other. Now have your friend run from right to left. If you throw the ball exactly where you see your friend at a certain moment, then the pass will be incomplete. Your friend has moved by the time the ball gets there. If you throw the ball a little ahead of where your friend is, with luck, the ball and your friend will arrive at the same place at the same time. It's a catch!

Getting to Mars is like playing catch with a football. Earth is you. The spaceship is the football. Mars is your friend. Earth must throw the spaceship a little ahead of where Mars is right now and get the two to arrive at the same place at the same time. If it happens you score a touchdown on the surface of Mars!

In space we can't afford any incomplete passes. Luckily, we don't have to guess how far ahead the spaceship must be "thrown." We know exactly how Mars is moving as it orbits the Sun. We know exactly how fast our spaceship can go. We also know exactly how gravity from Earth, the Sun, and Mars will affect the path of the spaceship. Scientists can use mathematics to figure out precisely the direction and speed a spaceship needs to get to Mars. It's not easy math, not like adding two and two to get four, but it's not too hard. Let's do just a little of this math.

As inhabitants of Earth, we are also in orbit around the Sun. It takes us 365 days to travel more than 580 million miles (934 million km) and complete one orbit. Mars, at an average distance of 141 million miles (227 million km), takes 687 days to travel almost 900 million miles (1,449 billion km) and complete an orbit. With these numbers we can find out how far each planet travels each day. All you have to do is divide the total distance traveled by the number of days. Dividing 580 million miles by 365 days tells us that Earth travels about 1.6 million miles (2.6 million km) per day. Mars travels about 1.3 million miles (2.1 million km); (900 million miles divided by 687 days) per day. Earth is traveling faster than Mars. In fact, the farther you are from the Sun, the slower you travel in your orbit.

To get to Mars we need to move from the orbit of Earth to the orbit of Mars. To leave the orbit of Earth, we must add energy to our orbit. We do this by firing rocket engines. As we start moving farther away from the Sun, we will actually slow down since the gravity of the Sun will be pulling on our spacecraft. Using our rockets again when we get to Mars, we must speed up a little so that we are moving at the right speed to stay in the same orbit as Mars. We call this path a **transfer orbit**.

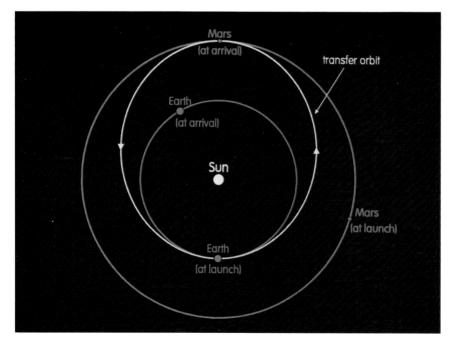

A transfer orbit between Earth and Mars. Spacecraft must be timed to arrive at the Mars orbit when the planet is at a specific location.

If we want to orbit Mars itself, we will have to slow down when we are near the planet. We can use rockets to do this or we can use the atmosphere of Mars. (We will talk more about this later on.)

We can't just go to Mars anytime we want. If your friend is too far away, you can't throw the football far enough to get it there. If you want to throw the football to reach your friend before another person can jump in and grab it, you might not be able to throw the football fast enough to get it there in time. You need to be able to throw it harder, which means using more energy.

A spaceship uses energy to move. The energy is made by burning fuel. You must carry enough fuel to produce the energy you need to get where you're going.

Once you get going in space, there is little to stop you. On Earth, **friction** with the air or ground slows down objects that are moving. More energy must be used to keep them going. In space there is no air, and you are not moving on a surface, so there is no friction to slow you down. The only thing that can slow you down in space is gravity.

Energy is needed to get you moving. The rockets that are used to launch spaceships from Cape Canaveral in Florida are using energy to get into space. Then the rockets stop. However, the spaceships keep moving. Most of them move in an orbit around Earth. When they want to come down, they need to use more energy. Rockets are used again to slow a spaceship so that it falls down to Earth.

To go to Mars, energy must be used to get the spaceship moving toward where Mars is going to be when the spaceship gets there. The rockets will stop once it is moving fast enough. When the spaceship gets to Mars, more energy must be used so the spaceship will fall into an orbit around Mars.

It takes a lot of fuel to get a spaceship moving fast enough to reach Mars. Getting there "extra fast" would use a lot more fuel. Then you need fuel to enter Mars orbit when you get there, more fuel to start back to Earth, and finally even more fuel to slow down when you arrive back in Earth orbit. That's a lot of fuel! To make room for all that fuel, the spaceship may have to be very large. Most of the spaceship will just be a big fuel tank. Also, the bigger the spaceship, the more fuel it needs to get moving. It's not easy to figure out how much fuel you will need.

Scientists can figure out the minimum amount of fuel needed to get a spaceship from Earth to Mars. This minimum use of fuel will cause the spaceship to travel along a transfer orbit. By noting various times a spaceship could take off from Earth and travel along this path, scientists can find the best times when the spaceship would meet Mars on its orbit. These times are known as **launch windows**.

Launch windows to Mars, using minimum fuel, occur about every two years. They last only a few weeks. These routes to Mars take about seven to nine months. Coming back will take just about as long. You have to wait for a launch window to come back, too. Because of the way Earth and Mars move in their orbits, a return launch window usually opens up very soon after arriving. That may only give you a few weeks on Mars—not much time to explore after such a long trip. The other option is to wait until the next window. That might mean you would have to stay on Mars for more than a year before coming home.

A round-trip to Mars, then, will take anywhere from nearly two years to more than three years! Would you be able to leave your family and friends for such a long time? Long ago sailors who visited the New World went on missions that lasted that long. Explorers have often had to spend long periods of time away from the people they know and love. To them, the rewards of adventure are worth it.

Will it always take so long to go to Mars? Maybe not. It depends really on what you use for fuel. Rockets today use chemicals for fuel. Hydrogen, oxygen, kerosene, and some aluminum compounds are common substances found in rocket fuels. Though inexpensive and easy to produce, they are not very good at producing large amounts of energy compared to some other possible fuels. In the future we may find other ways to propel us into space and toward Mars.

Back in the 1960s, while work was under way to send people to the Moon, scientists were also working on a new kind of rocket. It was called NERVA, which stood for Nuclear Engine for Rocket Vehicle Applications. This rocket used a nuclear reactor to burn hydrogen much more completely and with more heat than a chemical rocket. Scientists found that a lot more energy could be produced with much less fuel. This rocket engine was even tested several times in the Nevada desert.

Two views of the NERVA nuclear rocket engine being tested during the early 1970s.

In the 1970s the direction of the space program changed. Plans to visit Mars were put on hold. There was nothing for the NERVA rocket to do. Military officials looked at it for a while, but even they decided they weren't interested. The project was stopped. Recently some scientists have begun looking again at nuclear rocket engines. Because of the danger of radiation, they probably would never be used to launch a spaceship off of the surface of Earth. Once safely in space, however, they could be used to propel a spaceship toward Mars.

Astronauts would need protection from the radiation produced by these nuclear rocket engines. A shield of some kind would be needed between the crew area and the engines. These two areas of the spaceship might simply be placed at opposite ends of a long central section, possibly used for storage.

With the same amount of fuel as a chemical rocket, the nuclear engine would burn longer and could get a spaceship traveling much faster. The trip time to Mars might be reduced by a month or more.

Round-trip times might be only a little over one year! The path taken by a nuclear-powered spacecraft would not be a minimum energy transfer orbit, but since it can be plotted, scientists can also figure out when launch windows will exist for these missions.

For even longer missions to some of the outer planets like Jupiter or Saturn, nuclear engines would be even more important. Chemical engines would require many years to get a spaceship to these distant worlds. Nuclear engines could reduce that to less than two years. Much of the solar system might suddenly seem within reach.

Another method of propulsion has been tested in recent years. Electric fields can be used to speed up electrically charged atoms of a gas called **ions**. Aimed in a narrow stream behind a spaceship, they can act as a rocket. Moving at speeds of millions of miles per hour, they can eventually get spaceships moving at incredible speeds. The problem with electric field propulsion is that it speeds up a spaceship very slowly. These engines would have to operate continuously for many weeks. Experiments have shown this is possible. With an assist from chemical or nuclear engines, the addition of ion electric engines could further shorten the time it takes to get to Mars.

The first trips to Mars will use either the older chemical-style engines or nuclear engines. In order for trips to Mars to become commonplace, a new type of engine may be developed. Scientists are always looking for better ways to produce energy. Nuclear-fusion engines have been proposed that could take spaceships to Mars in only a few weeks!

Nuclear **fusion** is the way energy is produced in stars, including our own Sun. It involves atoms colliding with each other with great force. They combine and form larger atoms. In the process some of the mass, the stuff that makes up the atoms, is turned into energy. Even a very small amount of mass produces a large amount of energy. Albert Einstein discovered this and developed his famous equation: $E=mc^2$. In this equation, E is energy, m is mass, and c is the speed of light. The speed of light is a huge number: 186,282 miles (299,793 km) per second. This number is being squared, which means it is multiplied by itself. This produces a gigantic number. So a very small amount of mass produces a lot of energy.

Getting atoms to begin nuclear fusion requires very high temperatures and pressures. Scientists have not yet been able to produce a nuclear-fusion reaction on Earth that can continue to run on its own without adding more energy than is being produced by the reaction. Until they do, nuclear fusion is not terribly useful. If they eventually succeed, nuclear fusion could be the cleanest and cheapest way to produce huge amounts of energy. A nuclear-fusion spacecraft might be able to quickly gain very high speed. Even the most distant planets of our solar system would be only weeks away. Until that time traveling to the planets will probably remain a journey measured in months.

Missions using some of the launch windows to Mars are already planned using robotic spaceships. Trips have been proposed starting not long into the next century for humans as well. Launch windows using minimum energy transfer orbits are known far in advance, so planning can already begin. We are ready to plot our course to Mars.

WHEN WILL WE GO?

The long cables connecting the crew section of the space-craft to the cargo compartments and the nuclear engines have finally finished reeling out. There is now almost half a mile between the two sections of the ship.

Thrusters at both ends fire, causing the entire space-craft to spin. You find yourself floating slowly downward toward the floor. After a week of weightlessness, it feels strange to be experiencing gravity again.

Over the course of several days, the spacecraft slowly spins faster. Finally you find the gravity to be just about 38 percent of Earth's, exactly what you will find on Mars. It will remain like this until just before your arrival at Mars.

Earth and the Moon have now become just bright stars out the window. They are more than 5 million miles (8 million km) away! Still, there are many more millions of miles to travel to reach the red planet.

These first days have allowed you to become more accustomed to life in the spacecraft. You like your crew-mates. Working with them seems easy and fun. You hope it will always be this pleasant.

How soon might we be able to board our spaceship to Mars? That question is hard to answer because so many things must be done. Many decisions still need to be made. What kind of spaceship will we use? How long do we want to stay on Mars? How many people will go on the first trip? Scientists can figure out many possible ways to Mars. In fact, NASA (National Aeronautics and Space Administration) has done studies on different missions. There is no final decision yet on just when and how we will get to Mars.

Before we go, there will be many other robotic missions to Mars. These spacecraft will gather information that will help us decide the best place to land. They will also tell us more about the surface of Mars and what resources we could find there that could be used by a landing crew. They will prepare us for the Martian weather, possible Marsquakes, and other features of the planet. By making us more familiar with what we will find on Mars, these robotic missions will give us more confidence that we can send a spaceship with a human crew.

Mars Observer, launched in 1992, was to begin the process of preparation for the United States. This spacecraft was going to map the surface of Mars in great detail. Features as small as 5 feet (1.5 m) could have been seen. Unfortunately, for some unknown reason, the spacecraft stopped communicating with Earth just as it was about to enter orbit around Mars. This was a great disappointment, but there are other missions planned in the coming years.

The Russians, always very active in sending spacecraft to other planets, will probably launch several spacecraft during the late 1990s. These will include landers and orbiters. They may even attempt to bring Martian samples back to Earth. Included in the landers will be experiments from different countries. An instrument from the United States called the Mars Oxidant Experiment (MOX) will look for the chemicals in the soil that cause it to rust, giving the planet its reddish color.

Two of the possible landers are called penetrators and are shaped like spears. These will be launched from the orbiter like the landers but will reach the surface of Mars traveling at 300 miles (483 km) per hour. At impact they will break into two pieces. The lower section will bury itself several yards below the surface. It will look for Marsquakes and perform other experiments. The upper half will remain at the surface and monitor the weather and take pictures.

Russia is planning another mission that will include a small rover vehicle and a balloon. This will allow study for the first time of more than just the small patch of ground surrounding the lander. The rover and balloon both have cameras, and the airborne pictures from the balloon promise to be quite spectacular. The United States may send a very small microrover along for the ride. It may even be used to help guide the larger Russian rover if it gets stuck. The United States has now begun work on a mission called MESUR (pronounced measure), which stands for **M**ars **E**nvironmental **SUR**vey. Actually, this could become a series of missions, depending on the success of the first, called MESUR *Pathfinder*. This low-cost minilander will be launched in late 1996 and land on Mars by late 1997. Designed to be built quickly and cheaply, if it works well it may be followed in later years by groups of three or four MESUR spacecraft launched together. These would provide a network of stations on Mars relaying information about weather, soil chemistry, and geology.

Each MESUR spacecraft would include a camera and possibly a miniature rover, just 2 feet (.6 m) long, 1 1/2 feet (.5 m) wide, and 7 inches (18 cm) tall. The initial *Pathfinder* mission would be designed to last just thirty days. The later MESUR network would last much longer, perhaps for years.

The Japanese are now preparing to launch their first Mars mission, an orbiter scheduled for launch in 1996. The Europeans have canceled plans for a group of landers that would have been very similar to the MESUR spacecraft. Instead, several countries, especially France, are helping with the U.S. and Russian missions.

Though it seems a lot of missions to Mars are being planned these days, the first to have a human crew may still be a long way off. One of the biggest problems is cost. Costs for a trip to Mars have been estimated at anywhere from $10 billion for a mission relying on the use of many Martian resources for success to well over $100 billion for a mission that flies everything needed. Many are not sure it is worth it to spend that much money to visit another planet. They want to know what they will get out of it. Some people are not just worried about the cost. They wonder if we could make it to Mars and back safely. Others are not sure we should be going off and exploring other worlds when we can't even take good care of our own planet. Are we really responsible enough to explore Mars?

Safety is an important issue. How often do things around your house break? Has your television ever refused to work or has the car broken down during a trip to the supermarket? Luckily, there are stores and auto shops nearby where you can go to have appliances fixed or replace the things that break.

If you are in space traveling to Mars, there are no stores. There are no fix-it shops. Just millions of miles of empty space between you and the people who can help you. Unless you know how to fix what is wrong and have the parts to do the job, the broken part will remain broken. If it is something really important, like the air or water supply, you might not survive.

Having plenty of spare parts would help, but they take up space aboard the spaceship. There is only room for a certain amount. What do you take? What parts of the spaceship are you going to cross your fingers over and hope they don't break?

Looking back over the history of the space program, there certainly are some spectacular examples of disaster. The recent loss of the *Mars Observer* is a good example of the risks involved in going to Mars. In the past two other U.S. spacecraft and more than one dozen Russian spacecraft have failed to reach Mars successfully.

Other disasters have involved human life. In 1967 an Apollo spacecraft burned up on the launchpad killing three astronauts. Four Russian cosmonauts have died in accidents that have occurred during spacecraft recovery. In 1986 an explosion on the space shuttle *Challenger* killed seven astronauts, including the first teacher astronaut. All of these accidents involved minor problems that quickly got out of hand and led to major disasters.

Other examples, though, show how creative and intelligent people can solve what seem like major problems, even in space. In 1970 *Apollo 13* set off toward the Moon. Everything was progressing as usual until one night, as the astronauts were preparing to sleep, there was a sudden loud bang. An oxygen tank on their spacecraft had exploded, and they had lost most of the air they needed to survive. Quickly the three men scampered aboard the lunar landing vehicle designed to hold only two astronauts. They used the oxygen on this little craft to keep themselves alive until they could go around the Moon and get back to Earth several days later.

Back in 1962 John Glenn was orbiting Earth in the little one-person *Mercury 6* space capsule. Suddenly a warning light began to flash, telling him that his heat shield, which protected him during the hot reentry into the atmosphere of Earth, was loose. Identical indicators on Earth showed no problem with the heat shield. Glenn could not be sure whether his heat shield would hold or not but he knew that without it his spacecraft would burn up in a flash.

Before reentry he fired small rockets called retro-rockets. These rockets were held on the heat shield by straps attached to the capsule. Glenn and the mission controllers decided that instead of dumping the rockets after they had fired, he should leave them strapped on. The straps could then help hold on the heat shield, at least until the straps themselves were melted by the heat of reentry. Glenn successfully splashed down in the ocean. It turned out there was nothing wrong with the heat shield; but if there had been a problem, the quick thinking may have saved his life.

Robotic spacecraft have also had problems that have been solved or worked around by creative decisions here on Earth. Most spectacular of all may have been the odyssey of *Voyager 2*. This spacecraft was one of a pair launched in 1977 to travel to the outer gas giant planets of our solar system. *Voyager 1* was to fly by Jupiter and Saturn, taking the best path through both systems. *Voyager 2* would follow on a path not ideal for Jupiter and Saturn but giving it the option of continuing on to Uranus and Neptune. Shortly after launch, however, the main radio receiver on *Voyager 2* failed. The backup was switched on, but it too was not operating at its best.

Voyager 1 and 2 continued on their journeys. Fantastic encounters with Jupiter and Saturn by both spacecraft thrilled scientists. Right on course, the *Voyager 2* spacecraft continued on to Uranus. The only problem was that just after its encounter with Saturn, the moveable platform on which the science and camera equipment was mounted became stuck. The ability to move the platform was very important during the rapid flybys of planets. Only a few hours were available, and sometimes only a few minutes when looking at some of the moons. Because the spacecraft was moving so rapidly, the camera had to move to follow the worlds it was viewing in order to get a long enough exposure. It would be impossible to see everything if the problem with the platform was not fixed.

Mission controllers on Earth found that they could move the platform slowly. Afraid the platform might lock up completely or freeze, they decided to use only the slow speed of the platform and use the motion of the entire spacecraft to help move the platform. The controllers became so good at moving the whole spacecraft that they actually took even better pictures than those taken earlier using just the scanning of the platform. A problem had actually led to even better performance.

While we can never make traveling through space perfectly safe, the clever work of scientists and astronauts can make the risks smaller. Safety seems a goal within reach.

These days we hear a lot about the environment of Earth. Pollution of our air and water has become a major and expensive problem. The ozone layer, a gas high above in Earth's ionosphere that shields us from dangerous ultraviolet rays from the Sun, has begun to disappear because of certain pollutants released into the air. Forests of the world are disappearing forever as we continue to look for new places to live and work. Many people believe we are doing a poor job of managing our planet. They are worried the same thing will happen to any other world we attempt to live on.

Can we guard against the destruction of Mars? Do we really know how we will affect the planet by landing there? Let us hope that the first humans on Mars will remember not to litter or needlessly pollute the Martian atmosphere. Let us hope they will try hard to leave all as they find it, except for the samples of Martian soil and rock they will surely wish to bring back to Earth. We *can* do a better job of saving a planet. Scientists, the ones who have warned us about what we are doing to Earth, will be in charge of the exploration of Mars. They should be especially cautious!

The technology to go to Mars seems to exist. A likely launch date for the first mission will be about the year 2014. In the meantime, we can rehearse by traveling once again to the Moon. It has been over twenty years since the last Apollo spacecraft left Earth's nearest neighbor. Most of NASA's ideas for a trip to Mars involve a trial-run mission to the Moon. This would involve all the spacecraft and the same crew size that would fly to Mars. They would spend extra time orbiting Earth and the Moon to simulate the longer flight time to Mars. They would spend the same amount of time on the Moon that would be spent on Mars. They would perform similar experiments and travel on expeditions that would be like those of the Mars mission. If successful, we would know that a Mars mission could also succeed. If there are failures, the crew would have Earth only a short distance away to help.

A first mission to Mars will probably involve a shorter stay. Later missions will spend more than a year on the red planet. It will be twenty years or so before a permanent base is set up. Sometime after the year 2050 the first town will develop. By the year 2100 the population of Mars may reach one thousand! We can go to Mars when we want to but enough people have to decide the time is right.

There are still many steps to go before humans land on Mars.

WHAT DO WE TAKE WITH US?

It is now day seventy-four on the mission to Mars. The problem with the water recycling plant was fixed today. It's good to have all the fresh water you want.

You have been working on a new simulation program for the crew. As the computer scientist on the mission, it is your job to help keep the crew ready for what might be encountered on Mars. Using new information just received from the MESUR network on Mars, you have set up a new landing simulation that includes a geyser erupting under the spacecraft. It should provide an interesting challenge.

Still nearly one hundred days to go. Mars hasn't gotten any bigger than a bright star viewed from the windows. The thrill of adventure lies ahead of you. Coming back is going to be very hard. There will be months and months with very little to do. Hopefully, some interesting samples of Martian soil can be examined on the return flight. Or maybe some fossils of Martians will turn up!

Two of the crew gave a concert last evening of some original music they had written. It was quite good. They finished up with some old songs everyone knew, so you were able to sing along.

At the computer console in your cabin you ask for the library. Earth sent up a selection of new books yesterday. Maybe there is something you will find interesting to read in your spare time.

How would you spend eight months aboard a spaceship? Would you read many good books? Play video games? Take naps? Do you think you might get bored? The length of a trip to Mars is sure to be a problem for some people.

Most important is to have everything with you that you might need. There are no stores along the way for supplies. You will need to recycle many of the things you use everyday. Water and air cannot be wasted.

When we breathe, we inhale **air** that is made up mostly of nitrogen and oxygen. Our lungs remove some of the oxygen from the air to produce energy. In return, our bodies produce **carbon dioxide** as a waste product of burning up the food we eat with the oxygen we breathe. We release the carbon dioxide into the air as we exhale.

The air in a spaceship would slowly lose oxygen and become more and more filled with carbon dioxide. Our bodies cannot use carbon dioxide to produce energy. In fact, you would find it very uncomfortable to breathe in an atmosphere that had a lot of carbon dioxide. Something is needed to get rid of the carbon dioxide.

Spaceships today use chemicals to take the carbon dioxide out of the air. They also keep adding more oxygen into the air to replace that

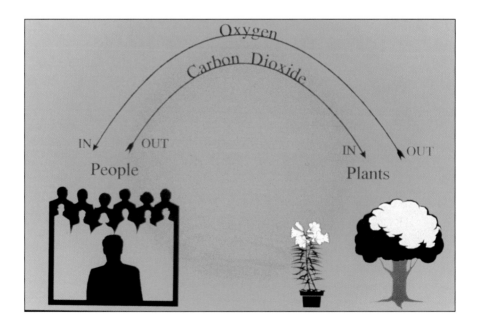

Plants and animals recycle the gases that make up Earth's atmosphere.

used by the astronauts. This works fine for short space trips or for orbiting space stations that can be resupplied with oxygen from Earth. Carrying enough oxygen and chemicals to keep the spaceship atmosphere fresh all the way to Mars would take up a lot of space and weight. There is a better way.

Air can be recycled using plants. Green plants use air almost exactly opposite from the way people do. Plants take carbon dioxide out of the air and convert it along with light into food. The waste product of this process is **oxygen**. We call this **photosynthesis**.

Growing plants aboard the spaceship to Mars would help keep the atmosphere fresh. Far fewer chemicals and stored oxygen would be needed, leaving more room for other equipment and supplies. The plants would also remind astronauts of life on Earth.

Plants have another benefit too. They can be used for food. Gardens could provide fresh vegetables and fruits for the crew, a welcome addition to the processed food used on most space flights today.

Long space flights to Mars should certainly include gardens. The benefits are great. Scientists would choose plants that are especially good at using carbon dioxide to produce oxygen as well as good food.

Water will also need to be recycled. Most spaceships today recycle at least some of the water on board. There are so many uses for water—to quench the thirst of a parched astronaut, for the plants, for washing clothes, equipment, and the astronauts, to cool the spaceship, to prepare food. Systems to remove dirt and other wastes from used water will be very important. Backup systems to make sure that water remains available in an emergency will also be needed.

How much water to take on the mission will depend on what the astronauts are likely to find on Mars. If a supply of water exists on Mars, the crew can reload when they arrive. Then only enough water for a one-way trip needs to be taken.

Water on Mars may also be used to supply another very important resource for the trip—fuel. Water is made up of hydrogen and oxygen atoms (H_2O, which means two atoms of hydrogen bonded to one atom of oxygen). Water can be split up to produce supplies of both these gases. Many chemical rockets work by burning hydrogen with oxygen. Nuclear engines will burn hydrogen. If our spaceship to Mars uses hydrogen with oxygen, then we might only take enough fuel to get us

Water is one of the most important resources for life. It will be crucial to any mission to Mars.

to Mars. Once there, we would need to set up a small factory to extract Martian water and separate it into hydrogen and oxygen. If the spacecraft engines are nuclear, then only the hydrogen would be needed for fuel.

The fuel provided by this factory could be used on Mars as well. Small electric power plants could be built that run on Martian fuel to power vehicles that would explore the surface of Mars. The oxygen would be used for providing air on the Martian base. Once set up, the fuel factories could continue to work and provide a ready supply of usable hydrogen and oxygen for later missions to Mars.

Many plans for the Mars mission suggest sending this fuel factory a few years ahead. Fully automatic, the fuel factory could be set up and working before the Mars crew is launched. By the time the astronauts arrive, a supply of hydrogen and oxygen could already be in place.

When the Mars crew is launched, a second fuel factory might come along to prepare another landing site for a future mission. Eventually, many of these factories might be scattered around Mars.

The spaceship to Mars must provide other things besides food, air, water, and equipment for exploring Mars. Crew members will need activities to keep them happy during the flight. Each astronaut is likely to bring along some hobbies to work on in his or her spare time. Fun group activities will be a regular part of the daily schedule. The crew will exercise every day to keep in good physical shape since much of the work on Mars involves moving around and carrying things.

The size of the spaceship will be important to the crew. Small living spaces make people feel cramped and uncomfortable. A full-size gym for playing team sports might be desirable.

What about **gravity**? We usually think of astronauts floating about in zero gravity. Spending six or seven months like this might not be very good for the astronauts. American astronauts aboard the *Skylab* space station during the 1970s spent up to eighty-four days in orbit without gravity. Upon return they suffered from weakened muscles. They even

Many things will be needed to keep the astronauts going to Mars healthy and happy.

found it difficult to stand. Russian cosmonauts aboard the *Salyut* and *Mir* space stations have spent up to a year in orbit. They have reported similar problems despite getting lots of exercise while in space.

Once on Mars astronauts will have to deal with gravity. Mars is a smaller planet than Earth, and the gravity on the surface is less than half of ours. However, after being weightless for so long, Martian gravity would make the astronauts feel very heavy. Therefore, some gravity during the trip to Mars would be a good idea.

The universe is made up of matter and energy. **Matter** is the stuff that everything is made of. **Energy** is actually something that all matter can be converted into. Energy is the potential ability of matter to do work. Forces control the way matter acts. One of these forces is gravity.

All matter has gravity. The more matter you have in one place, the more gravity you have. Earth is denser than Mars. That means the matter that makes up Earth is more tightly packed on average than the matter that makes up Mars. Earth is also almost twice as big across as Mars. This is why the gravity at the surface of Earth is more than twice the gravity at the surface of Mars.

When you drop something here on Earth, does it fall at a constant speed? No, it speeds up. Gravity is a force that makes matter speed up. On Earth gravity speeds up matter at a rate of 32 feet (10 m) per second. We usually write this as 32 feet/sec^2, which reads 32 feet per second squared. What this means is that each second a falling object will speed up. The falling object will be moving 32 feet per second faster. This increase in speed is called **acceleration**.

When you hold an object, such as a ball, it is not moving. Its speed is zero. When you drop the ball, after one second it will be moving at a speed of 32 feet per second. After two seconds it will have sped up, or accelerated, by another 32 feet per second, for a total speed of 64 feet (20 m) per second. After three seconds it will be moving 96 feet (29 m) per second; after four seconds it will be moving 128 feet (39 m) per second, and so forth.

On Mars the gravity at the surface is about 12 feet (4 m) per second squared (12 feet/sec^2). It would take almost three seconds for an object on Mars to reach the speed an object on Earth reaches in just one second.

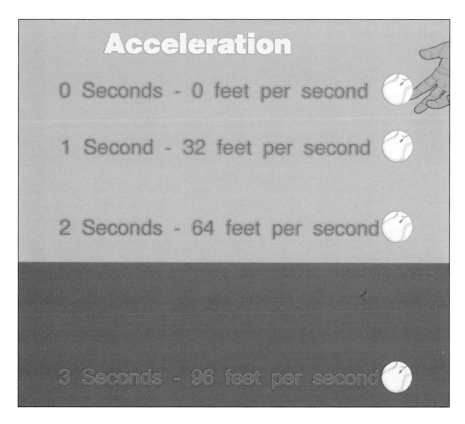

An object, such as a baseball, accelerates if it speeds up over time. The force of gravity is an acceleration.

While traveling toward Mars, the ideal way to prepare the astronauts would be for them to live in the same gravity they will find when they arrive. No machines exist that can produce artificial gravity. Many scientists think such a machine is impossible. That doesn't mean we can't give our astronauts any gravity. We simply need to find a way to make them feel accelerated toward the floor of their spaceship.

When you are traveling in a car and go around a corner, have you noticed how you seem to lean in the opposite direction from which the car is turning? It seems as if you are being pushed. Actually what is happening is that you are experiencing a battle between the changing direction of the car and your own **inertia**. If you are moving, or even sitting still, your body wants to remain in that state. This is inertia. Unless some other force acts on you, you should continue moving or sitting still. On Earth one of the forces we are affected by is friction. An object rolling across the ground is slowed by friction. If friction did not exist,

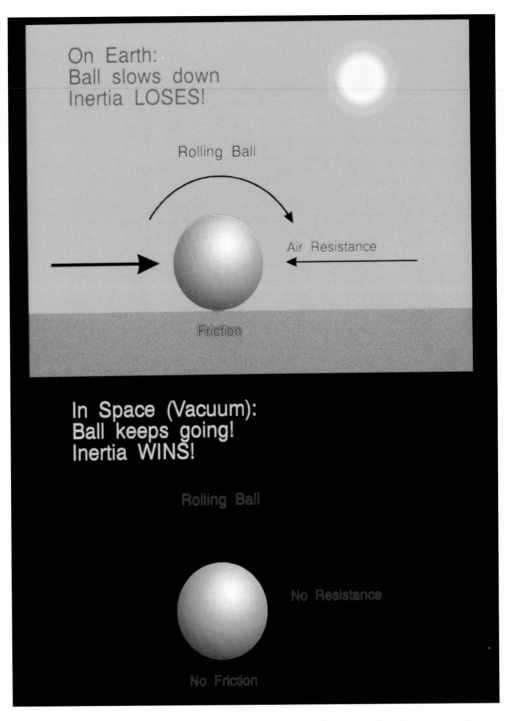

Inertia allows a spacecraft to continue moving through space without having its engines fire at all times.

the object would continue to roll forever unless something else got in the way to slow it down or stop it.

In space there is no air or surface to cause friction. The only force that slows down a spaceship is gravity. Unless a rocket is moving fast enough to get away from gravity, it slows down as it rises from Earth and will eventually stop and fall back to the ground.

On the way to Mars we have escaped the gravity of Earth. Our inertia will continue to take us outward toward Mars. The spaceship, the astronauts, all the equipment, food, and air are all moving at the same speed and with the same inertia.

But what if everything wasn't moving in the same direction? Go outside with a pail of water and swing it over your head very fast in a big circle. Does the water fall out and spill on your head? If the pail is moving fast enough, the water will remain in the bucket. As you swing the bucket in a circle, several forces act on the water. First, inertia makes the water tend to stay where it is. Since the water is in the bucket and the bucket is moving, the walls of the bucket move the water around. If you let go of the bucket and if there was no gravity to pull the bucket down to Earth, the bucket would continue in a straight line. The energy you are using with your arms to hold onto the bucket and swing it keeps the bucket and the water from flying away. The combination of all these forces results in the water traveling in the circular path of the bucket and not falling out onto your head.

We can perform a similar experiment with our spaceship. Imagine the crew living in a section of the spaceship that is at one end of the spaceship. If the spaceship is spun about the center of its length, then the crew will be like the water in the bucket. The faster the spaceship spins, the more force will be holding the crew against one side of the spaceship. Obviously, we would want that side to be the floor.

We don't want to spin the spaceship too fast. That could make the crew dizzy and sick. The longer the spaceship, the slower it would need to spin to produce the desired gravity. We might even use some kind of long cable connecting the crew section to the rest of the spaceship. This could be reeled out once the ship is under way and retracted when the spacecraft gets to Mars. With this kind of artificial gravity, the crew would be comfortable with the environment of Mars when they arrived. They would not have to waste time getting used to gravity

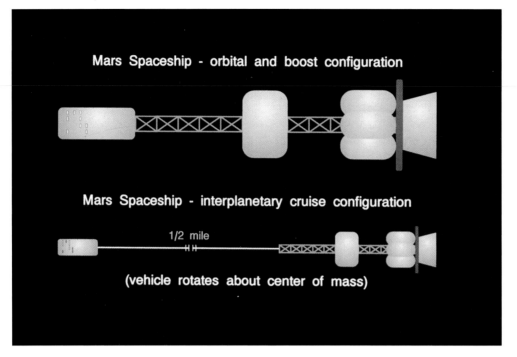

The spacecraft to Mars will probably be very large. In this illustration the crew will be housed in the section on the left. Landers are stored in the middle section. The fuel tanks and nuclear engines are at the right.

again. That would be a real advantage if the stay on Mars were only a month or so.

At this point we can probably begin to describe the spacecraft that will take us to Mars. Compared to the spacecraft that have been used to travel in Earth's orbit or to land on the Moon, the Mars spacecraft will be large. Even if we plan on using fuel gathered from Mars for the return trip, we will still need a fairly large ship to carry all the supplies and equipment that will be needed during the voyage out to Mars, on the surface itself, and during the return to Earth.

The first flight may use chemical propellants, but let us guess that a nuclear engine has been developed. It runs on hydrogen, easily acquired from Mars for the return trip. The nuclear fuels, uranium and plutonium, will have to be carried from Earth, but luckily only a fairly small quantity will be needed to power the engine.

The engine will be mounted at one end of a rather long tunnel connecting it to the crew section at the other end. In addition, the crew section will be reeled out about half a mile (.8 km) on thick, extra strong wire cables after the ship is under way toward Mars. The entire craft will then begin to spin about its center, producing gravity for the crew at the same level found on Mars.

Attached to the center of the tunnel will be the Mars landing craft. A heat shield will protect its bottom half for use when entering the Martian atmosphere. When the ship has slowed down enough, it will release the shield and fold out landing legs to be used on contact with the surface. A parachute and smaller rocket engines will help slow the craft even more for a gentle touchdown on Mars. Inside the landing craft is all the equipment needed for exploring Mars, including rovers, for traveling long distances across the surface. At the end of the stay on Mars, the upper half of the lander will blast off and return to dock with the main spacecraft.

The crew section of the main spacecraft will include plenty of space, with comfortable sleeping quarters for each member of the crew and ample recreation areas. There will also be a complete computer simulator on board that the crew can use to practice some of the work they will need to do when they reach Mars. This simulator will also be able to function as a sort of video game area for the crew, helping them to escape the boredom of the long flights between planets.

An observatory will probably be on board, with telescopes that will allow the crew to complete many experiments for astronomers on Earth. The many months of traveling will give the crew plenty of opportunity to perform experiments in many areas of science. Physical examinations will be a regular part of the crew's routine, and there will be a very good medical area on board. Various animals may be taken along, to serve both as pets and to gather information on how they adapt to the new environment of Mars as well as to the long journey.

The kitchen will be well stocked. Good food will not only keep the crew physically healthy but it will keep up their spirits. Each crew member will be allowed to order a supply of his or her favorite foods to be a part of the menu.

Lighting on board will simulate, as much as possible, the light we are used to on Earth. Main shipboard lights will probably fade and brighten in a 24-hour cycle, just as on Earth. This may gradually be adjusted to match the 24-hour, 37-minute day of Mars. Even seasons may be simulated, with longer days during summer and shorter winter days. Making as many things as possible seem Earth-like will help to prevent serious homesickness.

What will the typical day be like for an astronaut on the way to Mars? Mornings will begin pretty normally, with time for a shower, a good breakfast, and maybe a little exercise. Scheduled chores that need to be done around the spaceship will follow. Keeping things neat and clean will also be good for crew morale.

After lunch it is time for some experiments. A laboratory on the ship is filled with small stations at which each astronaut spends time working with other scientists on Earth. Some of them work on examining the Sun. Others gather information about distant star clusters. A comet may be nearby, an object everyone wants to see through the telescope.

Besides astronomy, other work is done in physics, biology, and even psychology. Some of this work is done on the space station in Earth's orbit, but the isolation of interplanetary travel gives special opportunities for study.

Dinner is a time for socializing. Attendance by the whole crew is expected, if not ordered, by the mission commander. Recreational activity in the evening will keep the crew happy.

The crew spends a good deal of time in simulation. Keeping their skills ready for the time they will spend on Mars is extremely important. Testing the astronauts every now and then will ensure that everyone is ready when the big day arrives.

Traveling millions of miles to Mars is a challenging mission, both in getting the spaceship ready and in choosing a crew who can work well together. Still about twenty years away, the first mission will wait until we have everything we need to make a successful flight possible.

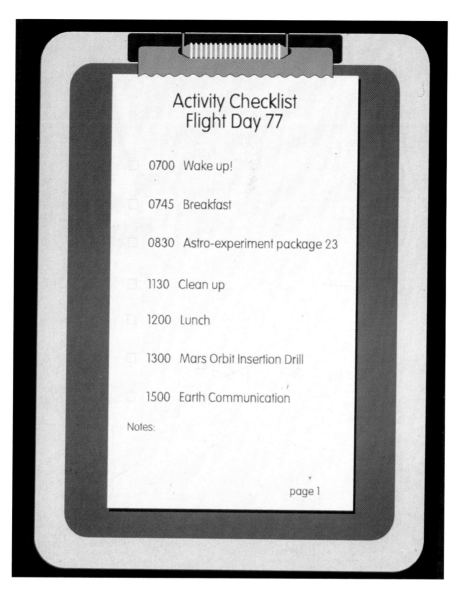

Activity Checklist
Flight Day 77

☐ 0700   Wake up!

☐ 0745   Breakfast

☐ 0830   Astro-experiment package 23

☐ 1130   Clean up

☐ 1200   Lunch

☐ 1300   Mars Orbit Insertion Drill

☐ 1500   Earth Communication

Notes:

page 1

There will be plenty to do for our adventurous Mars-bound astronauts.

WHO WILL GO?

Well, it is your day to prepare dinner. The kitchen aboard ship, known as a galley, contains many pieces of equipment that make preparing food easy.

First, you head to the supply locker. Here you find some chicken. It has been stored in a package without air called vacuum sealed, which keeps out anything that could cause the meat to spoil. That way it doesn't need to be refrigerated.

Then, you also collect some bacon, onions, and chicken stock. Finally, you find a bottle of white wine from which the alcohol has been removed.

Things can be cooked quickly in the well-organized galley. Less than half an hour later dinner is ready. The chicken is in a pot with the bacon, onions, chicken stock, and the wine. You have prepared some rice as well. Green beans help finish off the meal. Cookies and coffee or tea make up the dessert.

The chicken dish is called Coq au Vin, which in French means "chicken in wine." It was your specialty on Earth. You hope the crew likes it too.

When lots of kids get together at the park to play a team sport, the first thing that happens is that captains are chosen. These captains then take turns picking players for their teams. Of course the goal is to win, so the captains try to find players who will play well. The best players are chosen first, then later on the less-skilled players are added on. Sometimes it makes you feel bad to be picked near the end. You must remember that the captains want their team to be a success. Maybe if you practice hard and play well, you will be picked near the top another day.

In choosing a crew for the first mission to Mars, there will be many people who want to go but only a few who can. The first mission will probably have between four and twelve crew members. Those chosen to go must be the best and most skilled available. They will be scientists, explorers, and housekeepers, all rolled into one. Some will have to fill very special roles. If you want to be among the first chosen, you need to learn what skills will be needed and be sure to practice.

Life aboard a space station will provide good training for a mission to Mars. These NASA illustrations are based on plans for Space Station Freedom.

The crew will need to take care of themselves. Since they will be traveling so far from Earth, it will take many minutes for radio signals to travel between the spacecraft and mission controllers. Emergencies will have to be taken care of by the crew without help from Earth.

Physical condition will be an important factor in choosing the crew. Working on Mars will be hard despite the lower gravity. The crew will probably travel many miles to explore many different areas of the planet. Much of the work requires setting up and moving equipment or digging and collecting samples. Spaceflight itself requires people in good health to deal with the rapid changes in acceleration that occur during lift-off and landing on a planet.

Let's consider a crew of eight astronauts. Who will these people be? What kind of jobs will they perform on the way to Mars? What will they be required to do once the spacecraft has arrived?

Since a spacecraft is a vehicle, it needs someone to pilot it across space. Much of the navigation will be done from Earth, but having

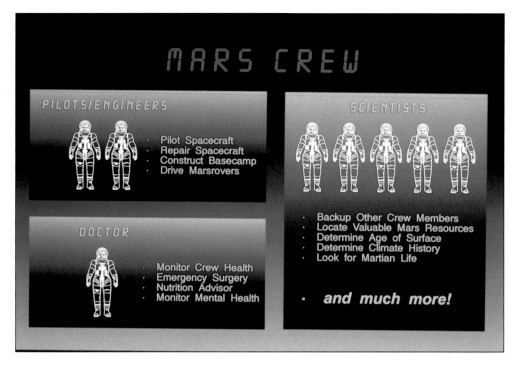

Each member of the Mars mission will have many duties. A successful mission will require lots of cooperation among the crew.

someone skilled on board is also essential. Landing a spacecraft on another world requires a pilot since signals from Earth will take five to twenty minutes to reach Mars. If the lander were to come down on the edge of a crater or cliff, only a pilot on the scene could react fast enough to prevent disaster. Once on Mars this crew will drive the rover vehicles on exploration missions across the Martian landscape. The crew will also serve as engineers, dealing with the mechanical problems that take place on the spaceships.

Setting up the base camp on Mars will fall to these crew members. Some of the equipment may be shipped earlier on the fuel factory spaceship that arrives ahead of the crew's spacecraft. The pilots will most likely have to retrieve this equipment as their first order of business after landing on Mars.

At least two crew members skilled in flying the spacecraft and lander will certainly be among the crew. One more will probably act as a backup if needed.

The long flight to Mars and back, along with the dangers of exploring a new world, makes it important to include a skilled medical doctor on board. Accidents will almost certainly occur, and there will be no hospital or ambulance available. Facilities for operations will be provided on board, including all the latest medical technology. The doctor will carefully monitor the health of the entire crew and be in charge of the nutrition of the crew, making sure the menu includes the required vitamins and other nutrients. Although the entire crew will probably help in the preparation of meals, the doctor may be trained as a chef as well.

The rest of the crew will consist of a variety of scientists. They must be able to explore many different areas of Mars. Scientists familiar with more than one branch of science may be considered better choices for the first missions.

A geologist may be the most obvious choice. Mars contains a great wealth of different landforms. There are massive volcanoes, deep canyons, cratered plains, polar caps, and more. Finding out when and how these different areas came into being will tell a lot about the history of Mars. Understanding more about the history of Mars may also tell us more about the history of Earth. Both planets were born in the same solar system from the same cloud of dust and gas that surrounded the Sun over 4.5 billion years ago. We can learn more about the formation of planets by learning how Mars formed and changed over time.

Marsquakes may also be found. The mission geologist will set up seismic stations looking for signs of activity beneath the crust of Mars. Most scientists believe Mars is less active than Earth. The great volcanoes seem to have stopped erupting as much as one billion years ago. There still may be some smaller eruptions on Mars, though.

There may also be a meteorologist collecting data on the local weather conditions and looking for signs of changes in the climate of Mars in the distant past. There are many scientists who believe that Mars was once far more Earth-like. If Mars was different long ago, maybe life could have once existed there. Some have suggested that Mars may be in an Ice Age. If the weather were to warm a good deal in some future age, melting polar caps could thicken the now very thin atmosphere. The addition of far more water vapor into the air may allow rains to fall. Dry riverbeds could once again be full. The crew will help search for signs of cycles in the Martian weather.

The possibilities for life make it likely that a biologist or paleontologist will be part of the crew. Paleontologists study ancient life. One of the things a paleontologist will look for among the rocks of Mars will be fossils, remains of life that lived long ago. Simple life could still exist in some regions of Mars—maybe near the northern polar cap, where a supply of water could be found, or in the floor of the great canyon, Valles Marineris, where morning mists indicate water vapor.

Collecting, sorting, and working with these data require a computer scientist on board, someone to design special computer programs to deal with the new data. This person may even help determine what kinds of data should be searched for among the various Martian landscapes. Instead of waiting until they return to Earth, the scientists will want to begin studying what they find immediately. The computer scientist can assist in this work.

Some discoveries on Mars may lead the team to decide to visit areas not planned by the original designers of the mission. The computer programmer will design simulations to help the team prepare for what they might find in these new areas of exploration.

A computer scientist would also be of use aboard ship since many systems on the craft will probably be computer controlled. A failure of a computer on the ship may need immediate attention, something controllers on distant Earth will not be able to provide.

Besides the work that needs to be done on Mars, the crew must assist each other in many chores around the spacecraft. Cooking and cleaning are part of each crew member's schedule. Keeping things neat will be important to the morale of the crew.

Both men and women will be on board. Astronauts from different countries may also be part of the crew. Friendships are certain to develop. At times problems between some of those on board may develop. The commander will be wise to solve these disagreements quickly so that they don't become long-term problems. The medical doctor may also be a skilled psychologist, ready to help the commander when problems between crew members arise or to help deal with cases of homesickness.

Not all decisions about the crew will be easy. More serious relationships might occur on the trip to Mars. Might crew members decide to marry? In the right circumstance, a married couple may even be chosen to fly to Mars, if both are qualified choices for the mission. Such close relationships could also make the long flight easier to bear. Of course, a serious problem between a married couple might hurt the mission. A real decision about this subject will not be made until more definite plans are under way for the journey.

In all, the Mars crew will need to be highly skilled, good-natured, flexible, and physically fit. They will have a long and difficult journey ahead of them, but one that will bring many rewards in the end.

WHERE WILL WE LAND?

6

Finally, you have entered the orbit of Mars. The view is incredible. All the pictures you have seen of Mars seem dull compared to the real thing. The vivid colors of the surface are very clear and sharp.

Overall, the planet is indeed red. Streaks of yellow and orange are common. Some areas are dark. There seems to be less dust and sand in these places. Near the polar caps you find white fields of ice. There are also a few areas that appear almost blue.

The landscape itself is majestic. The great volcanoes are so huge it seems you could stick your hand out the window and touch them. Just now a thin cloud is trailing off of the top of Olympus Mons. Valles Marineris looks like a giant gash in the ground, as if someone tried to carve the planet with a huge knife. Craters are everywhere, though they seem different from the ones on the Moon. They are flatter, and in some places seem to be fading. The atmosphere of Mars must be eroding these away, something that doesn't happen on the Moon.

It's hard to pull yourself away from the window. Much still has to be done before the landing, though. Soon the whole crew is busily getting ready for the adventure ahead. You feel incredible excitement. Soon you will have a chance to walk upon this strange new world!

After six to nine long months, the spacecraft approaches Mars. Everyone crowds around the view ports to examine the new planet they have come so far to see. Mars is beautiful after the long months of starry skies.

The spacecraft is still traveling rather fast. In fact, if nothing is done to slow it down, it will continue to zoom right past Mars. In order to fall into an orbit, the crew must find a way to slow the ship down. Rocket engines could be fired. This uses up fuel though and means that more fuel would have to be brought from Earth. Carrying that extra fuel would make the spaceship heavier and probably leave less space for equipment and experiments.

There is another way to slow down. Try dropping a coin into a swimming pool. As it is falling toward the water, it speeds up from the gravity of Earth. By the time the coin hits the water, it is moving quite fast. What happens when it hits the water? You should notice that the coin will slow down. It continues to sink in the water but not nearly as fast as it did through the air. Since the water is denser than the air, it is harder for things to move through water. So they don't move as fast.

A spaceship traveling through space doesn't even have air to move through. It can move very fast without being slowed down. That is why you might think that only rockets could slow a spaceship down.

However, Mars has something that can help. It has an atmosphere. The atmosphere of Mars is very thin compared to Earth's, but it is much thicker than no air at all. A spaceship could move very close to Mars. It would then enter the upper part of the Martian atmosphere. The air would act on the spacecraft like water on the coin. The spaceship would be slowed down. This is called **aerobraking**.

The slowing of the spaceship would also produce heat. This comes from the friction of the air rushing past the speeding spaceship. Try rubbing your hands together very fast and you will feel the heat from friction. The spaceship will need some kind of heat shield to protect it.

As it approaches Mars, the ship will stop rotating and the long cables will be retracted. Gravity aboard ship is reduced to zero. Then a heat shield will be set up of a strong inflatable material that could form a disk-shaped balloon in front of the spacecraft. Slowing down this way may be rough, so the crew will want to strap in for the ride.

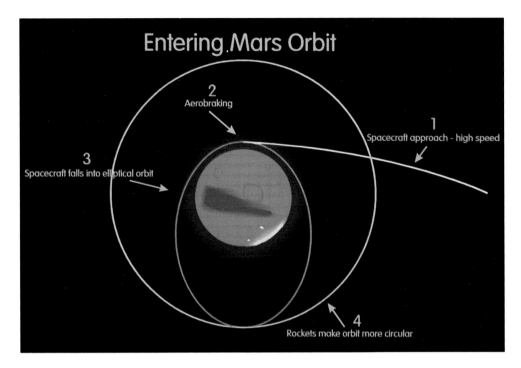

Entering Mars Orbit

2
Aerobraking

1
Spacecraft approach - high speed

3
Spacecraft falls into elliptical orbit

4
Rockets make orbit more circular

Getting your spaceship into orbit around Mars will require extremely careful calculations and piloting skills.

A few minutes later the spacecraft would skip back out of the atmosphere like a flat stone skipping across a pond. The ship will be traveling much slower now and will be able to enter orbit around Mars. Now the crew must prepare to land.

The decision about where to land may be made even before the mission leaves Earth. If a fuel factory/cargo spacecraft is launched ahead of the crew, then they will want to land nearby. Even if the astronauts have brought everything with them, the choice of a landing spot may have been previously chosen to give them the best possible situation in which to begin their exploration.

The landing location will be one that can provide access to areas picked for exploration, as well as contribute some of the resources such as water that they will need. The work already done by *Mariner 9* and the Viking spacecraft has given us some indication of where these areas might be. Other robotic spacecraft that arrive before this first mission with crew will help make the final decision.

The primary goal of the first mission will be to get to Mars and return safely. Decisions will keep that goal firmly in mind. If disaster were to strike, it would be difficult to convince many people on Earth that the risks were worth the long distance and great expense needed to reach Mars. Therefore, the first landing will take place in what is thought to be a very safe location. A flat plain with no large craters, cliffs, or mountains will be chosen. If possible, this location will be within reach of some of these other locations using the rover vehicles that will be used on Mars. If not, the first expedition may have to be satisfied with less than the perfect choice of exploration sites.

These very thoughts were in the minds of the mission controllers who commanded the landings of the Viking spacecraft in 1976. They searched through the pictures returned by the orbiter spacecraft seeking ideal, safe-looking locations to land. Yet when the landers set down and the first pictures were returned, the locations that had looked so safe from orbit turned out to be rocky plains, littered with rather large boulders. In fact, *Viking 2* was leaning to one side, one footpad apparently resting upon a large rock. Disaster could have taken place, and no one would ever have known why.

Finding these safe landing spots will take some detailed searches by both orbiting and landing spacecraft. The many missions planned for the next decade and beyond will set the stage for this eventual astronaut-led expedition.

Even if the first Mars mission brings along all the water needed, the ship will probably land near a source of Martian water. Not only will this be a backup water supply but such a location is the best place for present or past life on Mars. Many floodplains have been identified on Mars and many dried river channels cross the surface. These will be near the top of the list for landing spots.

A few of the pictures returned by earlier spacecraft have included what appear to be geysers bursting from the Martian surface near some of the large volcanoes. This is a clue that vast supplies of water may exist trapped beneath the red soil. If water is near the surface, it may be possible for the explorers to tap into this supply.

Geysers are also an indication that there is still some geologic activity on Mars. On Earth, geologic activity includes such occurrences as volcanoes, earthquakes, and the slow drift of continents. It also produces fields of geysers, like those found in Yellowstone National Park.

Geysers are produced by pressure and heat beneath the surface of a planet turning liquid water into steam that expands and forces its way explosively to the surface.

When planets are formed, they are mostly molten rock beneath a thin crust. Over millions of years the planet cools, and the crust begins to thicken. Smaller planets will cool more quickly than larger planets. Since Mars is about half the diameter of Earth, most scientists believe it has cooled far more than Earth.

Volcanoes occur where molten rock from beneath the crust bursts up through cracks in the crust. If the crust is thick, it will be hard for molten rock to reach the surface. On Earth, the crust is only about 4 to 40 miles (6 to 64 km) thick. Molten rock can still make its way to the surface, producing the many active volcanoes we find on our planet.

On Mars many volcanoes have been identified, including massive Olympus Mons, the largest volcano ever found in the solar system. However, most of these clearly have not erupted in millions of years. The crust of Mars must have thickened far more than Earth's. The existence of geysers would indicate some heat is still reaching the surface. Some smaller volcanoes may be active on Mars as well.

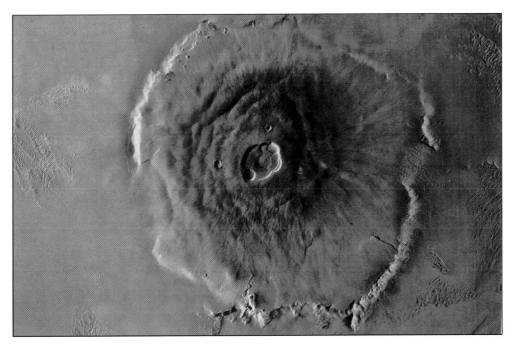

The huge volcano Olympus Mons. The impact craters near the summit indicate that the last eruption was millions of years ago.

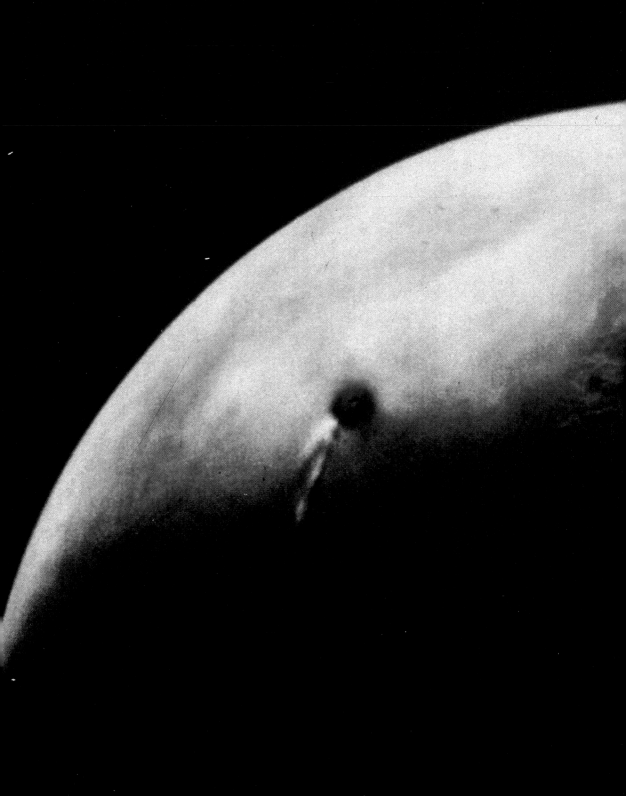

The first approaching visitors to Mars may be greeted by this view.

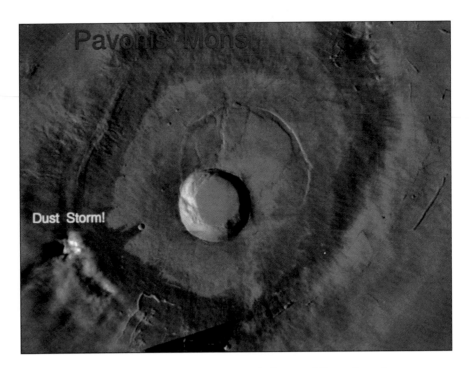

The circular crater on the volcano Pavonis Mons looks very different from the craters on top of Olympus Mons and Ascraeus Mons. Dust storms are a frequent feature of Mars and can, at times, cover the entire planet.

Earthquakes occur when motion of the molten rock beneath the surface causes the crust above to slip. These most often occur on Earth where great floating plates of crust are in contact with each other, with the two plates moving in different directions. These plates carry continents across the Earth. Over millions of years the continents shift position. This is known as **continental drift**.

Scientists would be very interested to know if this ever happened on Mars or may even still be occurring today. They will set up seismometers, devices that can detect Marsquakes. Some evidence, such as the massive size of some of the volcanoes, indicates that the plates probably have not shifted much. This would allow the surface to remain stable over a single hot spot for a long time and build up these giant volcanoes. Studies of Marsquakes and other geologic activity will help solve the mystery.

The weather on Mars may also affect the landing. When *Mariner 9* arrived on Mars in 1971, a giant, planet-covering dust storm was in progress. These dust storms occur every few years on Mars and would

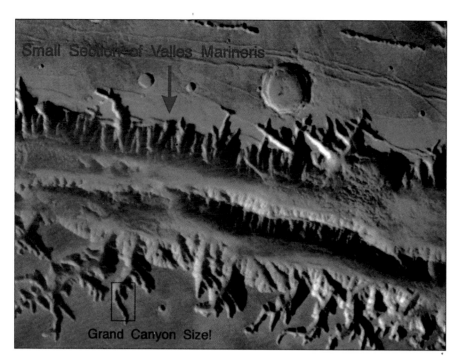

Small Section of Valles Marineris

Grand Canyon Size!

The huge size of Valles Marineris is best appreciated when you compare it to the size of something here on Earth, such as the Grand Canyon.

certainly present a hazard to a landing spacecraft. Should a large dust storm be under way on Mars when the spacecraft arrives, it may be necessary to postpone a landing. If the spacecraft needs to begin its return to Earth within a couple of months, this could be a problem— especially if the fuel for the return flight is on the surface in a fuel factory launched ahead.

These dust storms seem to be associated with the change of seasons on Mars. The arrival of spring in the southern hemisphere causes evaporation of frozen carbon dioxide (dry ice) producing powerful winds that blow toward the north. These winds carry the loose dust covering much of Mars high into the atmosphere. The dust remains suspended there for long periods of time. In fact, the Martian sky appears orange because of all the dust found there.

The first mission to Mars will be carefully timed to avoid this season. Still, smaller dust storms can arise at any time. Several landing sites may have to be chosen if dust is a problem at the ideal location. It will still have to be within reach of the fuel factory.

The best landing site will probably be somewhere on a flat plain between the region of Mars called the Tharsis Ridge and Valles Marineris. The Tharsis Ridge is a high plateau on which the largest volcanoes of Mars are found. Valles Marineris is the one huge canyon that actually may have been one of the canals seen by Schiaparelli more than one hundred years ago. This site offers access to very different and fascinating features.

The expedition will want to visit the north polar cap if there is time. If the stay on Mars is limited, a later mission may land near the cap. If a supply of water is needed and no definite source can be found outside the polar cap, then the first mission may land there instead. This, however, would make it more difficult to see other areas of Mars.

Recently scientists have found signs of a great flood on Mars. This occurred long ago in an area called Argyre Planitia, a large circular plain about 500 miles (805 km) across, surrounded by mountains. It

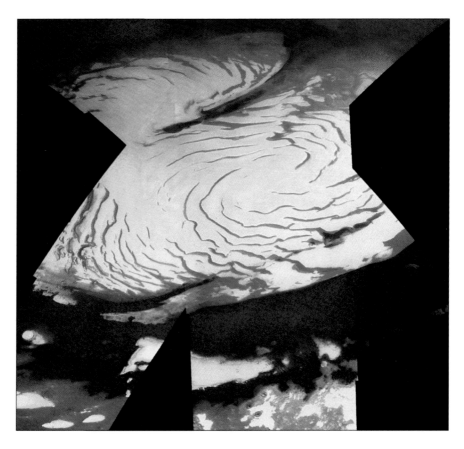

The north polar cap of Mars. Scientists believe that much of this cap is made of water ice.

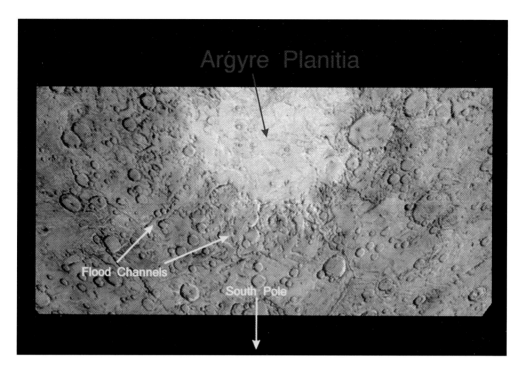

Argyre Planitia

Flood Channels

South Pole

This photograph shows an old impact crater, Argyre Planitia, located near the Martian south pole. There is evidence that great floods from the south have spilled into this crater in the distant past.

is actually a crater filled with dust. Signs remain of large amounts of water flowing from the area of the southern polar cap around the mountains of the southern end of Argyre. The water then flooded the plain before flowing back out through the mountains at the north. Maybe some of the water is still trapped beneath the floor of Argyre.

This is another site that may be visited. We will want to find out how long ago this flood occurred. How long did the plain remain flooded? Could life have begun in this temporary ocean on Mars?

One of the features of Mars seen by the Viking orbiters is especially strange. Over 1,000 miles (1,610 km) northeast of Valles Marineris is a group of hills. Many of these have the shape of a pyramid. Another appears to look like a human face staring straight up into space. Most scientists believe these are natural features, carved out of rock by wind and sand. Others are not so sure. A group of scientists has used the Viking data to make a computer model of the face. They have even improved the image a little using their computers. They

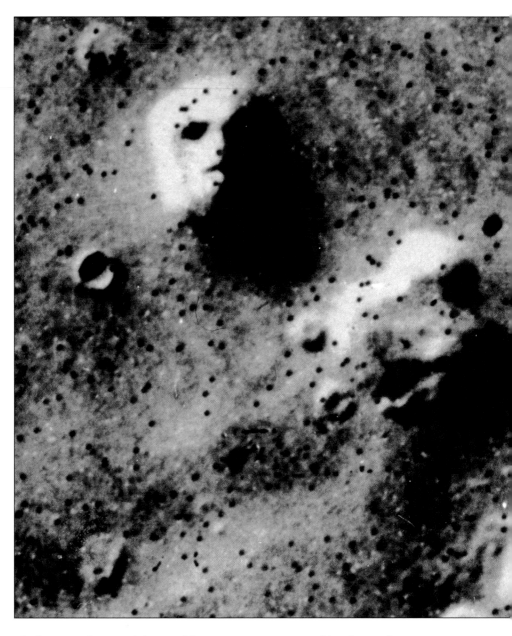

The feature in the upper left part of this image appears to resemble a human face. Was it formed by winds or by the hands of intelligent beings?

believe the face and pyramids should be looked at again. Imagine if they turned out to be the remains of another intelligent race of beings. Were they born on Mars? Or did they arrive from somewhere deep in space and visit Mars the way we are planning to do? If future space

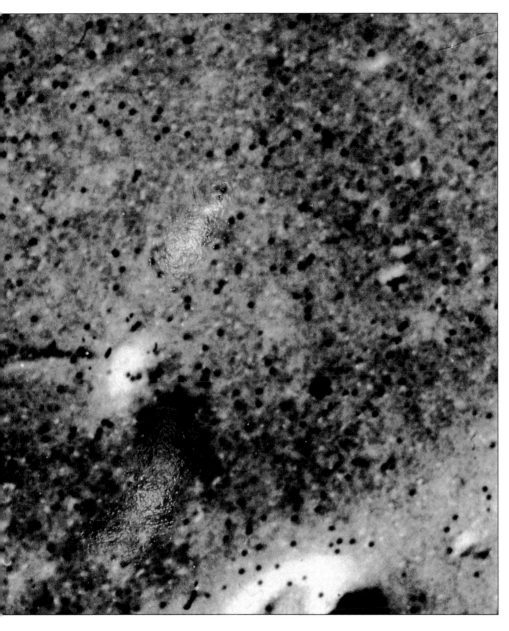

probes indicate this may be the case, expect the first crew mission to Mars to head for this region. Signs of alien life are sure to be considered the most important thing to see.

These are only a few of the interesting places to visit on Mars. Others will surely be found. No matter how long the astronauts spend on Mars, it will always seem like there is so much more to see. It will take more than just one or two missions to really learn what Mars is like. Hopefully, many explorers will have the chance to travel to the red planet.

WHAT WILL WE DO ONCE WE GET THERE?

7

Everyone is strapped into the Mars lander and ready to go. With a small KERCHUNK you feel the lander separate from the main spaceship as you begin your journey down to the surface. Entering the atmosphere causes the lander to rattle around rather roughly, but it is not nearly as bad as you remember reentry on Earth. The commander assures the crew that everything is going well and that the landing is only a few moments away.

You feel a sudden jerk as a parachute is released to help slow the lander. The rapid change in speed makes you sink into your seat. Since preparing for entering the orbit of Mars, you have been weightless because the spacecraft was no longer rotating at the end of the long cables. Now you feel the first gravity in over a week.

The commander warns you to hold on. It's time to fire the landing rockets. The parachute is released, dropping the lander into a free-fall. It seems like your insides are rising right up through your throat. Then the rockets fire. SLAM! You are right back into your seat again.

The rockets fire with slight changes in thrust as the commander scans the surface for a smooth landing site. Just moments later you feel a slight bump as you settle safely onto the Martian ground.

The thrill of being the first to land on Mars makes the long journey worthwhile. Stepping out onto the landscape of another planet, the explorers face many challenges and a great deal of work.

Until a base camp can be set up, the crew will live on board their landing vehicle. With all the equipment and supplies, it will be very crowded. They will not waste any time getting the base camp together.

A large dome filled with breathable air will be the home base camp for the astronauts on Mars. Inflated like a balloon, patch kits will be scattered around the edges to cover any leaks that occur. The material itself may be transparent so that a clear view of the Martian landscape is always available.

Getting outside requires an air lock. Air locks are used on space-ships to let an astronaut move from inside a pressurized spacecraft with breathable air to a poisonous environment outside. An air lock is like a small room with two doors. Only one door can be open at a time. An astronaut in a space suit goes from the base into the air lock. Once the

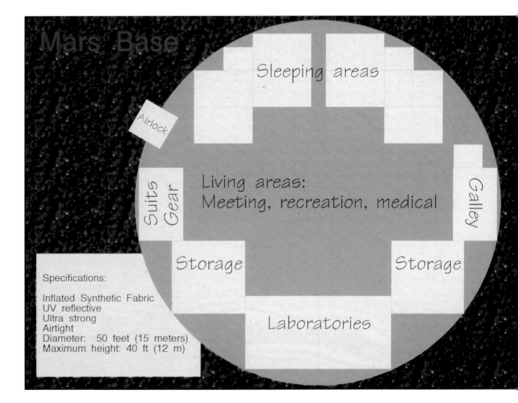

One possible floor plan for an inflatable Mars base.

astronaut closes the door behind himself or herself, the air lock then slowly moves out the air from the base and replaces it with air from outside. Then the outer door opens and the astronaut steps out onto the surface of Mars.

Before inflating the base camp air dome, the crew will move most of the supplies inside. That way they will not have to use the air lock, which would slow down the process. It would be like putting groceries into a giant bag. Once most of what they needed was inside, they would inflate the dome-shaped structure. Then they could all pass through the air lock to get inside and start setting up their new home.

Each astronaut would, of course, have his or her own sleeping area. There would be a kitchen and bathroom and a meeting area to discuss plans for exploration. Laboratories would be set up to begin examining some of the samples that are collected from Mars They would have an area set aside for packaging samples that would be returned to Earth. They would also set up a radio antenna for communicating with ground controllers on Earth. A large part of the base camp would be used for the storage of supplies and equipment.

When the base camp is set up, it will be time to begin exploring Mars. First the astronauts will stay close to the base, collecting samples to be kept in case they have to make a quick return to orbit because of an emergency. It would be a shame to travel all this way and leave empty-handed.

A seismometer will be set up. This is a device that can detect and record Marsquakes. They will also set up a small weather station. Computers will monitor the equipment and alert the crew if anything unusual happens.

Since the search for life, past or present, is the most exciting investigation for the crew, the first long-distance trip will likely be to Valles Marineris or to an apparent riverbed or floodplain. Here the explorers would search for signs that water did indeed flow here in the past. They may drill beneath the surface for signs of water still in the area. Rocks and soil will be carefully examined, with the astronauts looking for even the smallest living microbes or fossils of life that existed possibly more than one billion years in the past.

Weather and seismometer stations will be set up here and at every location the crew visits while on Mars. Before returning to Earth, they

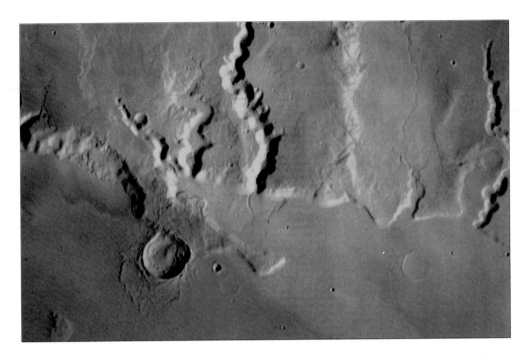

This ancient shoreline might be a good place to search for fossils of extinct Martian life.

will have established a long-term system to monitor conditions on Mars. This will aid future missions in determining new areas of Mars to explore.

After a brief return to base and some time to rest, the exploring team will head off to one of the Martian volcanoes. A climb to the top is unlikely because of the time and danger involved. Instead they will sample areas along the edges and sides of the volcano, seeking information on past eruptions. Old lava flows will be studied. Since much of the atmosphere of Mars may have come from gases released during eruptions of volcanoes, the lava could give some clues as to how thick the Martian atmosphere was in the past.

An eruption is very unlikely. Pictures of the volcanoes from *Mariner 9* and the Viking orbiters indicate that eruptions on Mars stopped long ago. Still, the astronauts on Mars may be able to tell if any volcanoes are likely to erupt again in the future.

If time and distance allow, a trip to the north polar cap follows. Here may be found a record of climatic change on Mars going back millions or billions of years. Samples of the ice cap can tell us how much of the ice is water and how much is frozen carbon dioxide. Knowing how much total water exists on Mars could tell us whether rivers, lakes, and even oceans ever existed on the planet.

On Earth the climate, the general pattern of the weather, has changed many times in the past. At times our planet has become much colder, and great ice sheets have covered large areas of our world. These times are known as Ice Ages. Could the same thing happen on Mars? Maybe Mars is in an Ice Age right now. If there is a cycle to the climate on Mars, will the temperature warm up again in the future? Would more of the water ice melt, thickening the atmosphere? Could rivers and oceans exist again some day?

Some of what the astronauts learn as they travel about on Mars may be used in the future to change the planet. Instead of waiting for natural climatic change, there may be ways that we could warm the planet ourselves. We could melt the polar caps by using large orbiting mirrors to reflect sunlight. Scattering dark material on

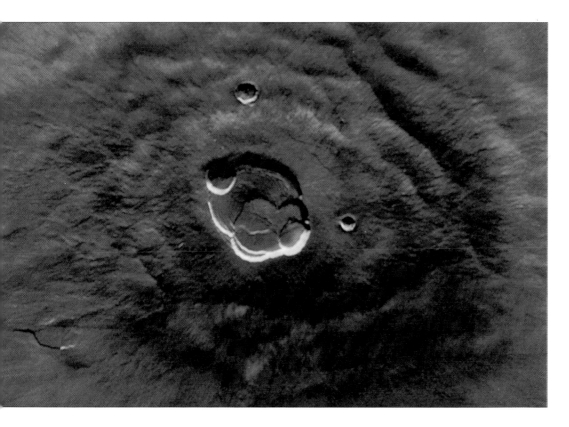

Geologists will be eager to explore Olympus Mons and the other Martian volcanoes.

the bright ice would allow more heat to be absorbed into the ice, melting it more rapidly.

Melting the polar caps would pump both carbon dioxide and water vapor into the Martian atmosphere. A thicker atmosphere could help astronauts immediately. They might no longer need bulky space suits. If the atmosphere became thick enough, they could use simple oxygen masks over regular clothing while exploring. This would make many tasks easier.

Carbon dioxide and water vapor are known as "greenhouse gases." A greenhouse gas is very good at absorbing heat but very bad at letting it escape. As sunlight enters the thicker atmosphere of Mars, it would become heat when it strikes the surface. The greenhouse gases will not allow the heat to escape. The planet would warm up even more, and even more ice would melt. The warmer temperatures and supply of carbon dioxide might allow plants to grow on the Martian surface.

Plants would convert some of the carbon dioxide to oxygen. Over a long period of time, probably at least several hundred years, the atmosphere might support some animal life. Even humans might be able to breathe the Martian atmosphere directly, at least for short periods.

The process of changing a world to make it more Earth-like is called **terraforming**. Is it right to make such a drastic change in the natural condition of another planet? If some simple life-forms do exist on Mars, they must be considered as well. Changing the conditions on Mars may be poisonous to them. They might not be able to survive with life-forms from Earth.

Only if Mars is a totally lifeless, or sterile, world would terraforming be considered. Otherwise, Martian life must be preserved as much as possible. Maybe what we learn while trying to save endangered life here on Earth can help on Mars.

When the time to leave Mars nears, the crew begins packing up. Some of the equipment is left behind, such as the rover vehicles and monitoring stations. Important samples are carefully labeled and packaged for the long journey to Earth. After packing the lander, the base itself will be collapsed. Instead of returning it to Earth, it is carefully packaged and left behind for possible use by another Mars landing mission.

The crew says good-bye to their home on Mars and climbs aboard for lift-off. Returning to their orbiting spacecraft, they are met in orbit by a fuel tanker from the factory on the surface. Once refueled, they fire the rocket engines and start the return flight to Earth. On the way they continue their studies of the Martian samples. They may establish communication with another astronaut mission already on its way to Mars. The next crew of explorers benefits from the experiences of the first to work on the surface of the red planet.

CAN WE DO IT?

Getting into your space suit is hard. Not only is it complicated but you are so excited that your hands are shaking too much to zip and snap the various parts of the suit.

The commander is the first to enter the air lock. Shortly afterward, you hear the machinery grinding as the outer door opens. Someone is out on Mars! Finally, it is your turn. It only takes a few moments to clear the spaceship air and fill the air lock with the atmosphere of Mars. Then the green light above the door comes on. You press the button next to the door, and it begins to open. Not long ago the Sun rose, and it is almost directly in front of you, scattering its light upon the red ground. Long shadows are cast by the many small rocks and larger boulders that are strewn about. Most striking, though, are the shadows cast by the other members of the crew. They all seem frozen in place, standing about on this wonderful new world.

Stepping onto the ground, you suddenly feel like running. After so many months in the spaceship it is a relief to be out in the open. "How about a game of baseball?" you ask.

Everyone laughs.

Going to Mars certainly sounds exciting. Many people would love to see humans go. Still many others, though, do not support the idea of going to Mars. This includes many of the people in positions of power in this country. Until they believe in going to Mars, the adventure will have to wait.

Why doesn't everyone support a mission to Mars? Mostly because of the cost. At the time of the Apollo landings on the Moon in the late 1960s, there were some who tried to guess how much it would cost to go to Mars. A figure of $100 billion was estimated. Because of inflation, that would be much higher today. Numbers like this are very scary to people who must decide how to spend the country's money. All work on a Mars mission stopped.

The problem is not that all plans for going to Mars are so expensive. More recent NASA studies suggest it could be done for about $40 to $70 billion. That is still a lot. Other independent companies and universities have also studied the problem and have come up with programs that are much cheaper. Some of these programs present greater risks. Many people think going to Mars is not worth the risk.

What will be accomplished if we go to Mars? Many think we will get nothing out of spending all that money. They see it as a waste when there is so much to do right here on Earth. Is there anything to gain by going to Mars?

Cost? Risk? Value? These are the three big questions that have stopped us from going to Mars. Interestingly, no one seems too concerned about the technology needed. The reason is that most of the technology already exists and has existed since we landed on the Moon. We really only need a reason and a will to go.

What about the cost? Can a Mars mission be had for a "bargain" price? Can we afford even the simplest mission? Are the risks too high? Can anything important and valuable be guaranteed?

Estimates on going to Mars today range from $10 to $400 billion. By comparison, the United States Defense Department spends almost $300 billion every year training soldiers, building bombers, and developing top-secret projects.

The cost of going to Mars would be spread out, probably over more than ten years. Spacecraft will have to be designed, built, and tested.

Astronauts will need to be selected and trained. Planning of landing sites and experiments will need to be done. The cost per year will be more like $3 to $15 billion. That is quite a bit less than we spend on defense, welfare, and social security. It's less than is spent by Americans each year on cigarettes and alcohol.

Any mission to Mars will, of course, be risky. There is so much we don't know about travel in deep space. The unknown landscape of Mars could offer many dangers. The equipment and spaceships are bound to suffer failures on such long flights between worlds.

However, as has been shown in the past, our technology can help us deal with and overcome many difficulties. Good preparation will go a long way to avoid serious problems on the way to Mars.

What will we come back with? "Rocks," you say. "Maybe some ancient fossils from long dead life-forms." Is it worth it?

Mars represents a frontier. There are few other frontiers left on Earth. We have explored and colonized all of our planet except for the ocean floor. One of the only places left to make discoveries is outer space. In history there are many examples of what can happen during the exploration of frontiers. There are risks involved; it can be costly at times, but in the end there have been great rewards. Ignoring a new frontier can also be costly.

In the fifteenth century the Chinese built a fleet of large ships, among the greatest on Earth. They were the most important power on the seas. They traded in expensive spices collected from the islands of the Far East. The fabulous riches they brought back to China allowed all the people to prosper. It may have been the best time in the history of China. Then the Europeans arrived in the Far East. They sailed in much smaller ships and were not well trusted by the other nations of the area. They were only minor players in the spice trade.

The Europeans also brought with them new ideas and customs. These were seen as very foreign and even dangerous by the rulers of China. The Chinese emperor and court feared that the spice fleet might bring some of these unwelcome customs and ideas to China. They decided to destroy the Chinese spice fleet and commanded the traders to remain at home. The riches stopped flowing into China. Soon the wealth of the nation dried up, and China dropped into a long dark age.

The Europeans, meanwhile, without competition from the better-equipped Chinese, took over the spice trade, becoming powerful and rich themselves. It was one of the events that helped to end the long dark ages that had been in place in Europe for over five hundred years. In effect, the Chinese stopped dreaming about what they could learn and do by exploring. Without dreams, they lost direction. The people suffered.

Do we have dreams today? Do we know where we want to go and what we want to accomplish? Some people in America are worried that we do not have goals and that our children don't know what to look forward to. Could Mars be a goal?

As far as we know, there are no valuable spices on Mars, but there could be other valuable resources waiting for us, or someone else, to discover. Even without valuable resources, frontiers can offer other riches. A place to build new industries and homes has to offer the basic necessities of life. Mars has these.

As we've already seen, water and air can be found on Mars. Since people can, with a little work, live on Mars, they probably will. They will explore and colonize the planet.

There are other benefits to exploring and colonizing frontiers. It provides jobs to people who are not actually involved in the exploration. People are needed to build spaceships, plan the expeditions, collect and provide supplies, and train the explorers. These people also require others to provide services that in turn create more jobs.

Traveling in space is a highly technical job. People working in this field are well educated and make a lot of money. They pay taxes that help make our country work. They need other people to work in other service jobs to support the needs in their lives.

When the Soviet Union fell apart and the United States Defense Department cut back on building new and expensive weapons systems, lots of people lost good, high-paying jobs. These people are the same type of people who can help design and build a program to explore Mars. If instead of letting them work at lower-paying jobs, or even no job at all, we started on a determined plan to reach Mars, that would be good for all of us!

In school young people would see and learn about other worlds. They would know that it takes a good education to succeed at exploring such worlds. These possibilities are very exciting and could give a student a reason to want to do well in school, so that he or she can also join in the adventure.

Going to Mars will be difficult, dangerous, and fairly expensive, but some people will no doubt eventually go there. Who will these lucky people be? I hope it is you and me! Just imagine what it will be like.

AT THE EDGE
OF THE VALLEY

The next four chapters describe an imaginary exploration of Mars. Here are some of the adventures that might await you on the red planet.

The first expedition away from the base camp begins today. The mission commander will drive the rover. The biologist and geologist will go along. You have been asked to accompany them as well. As computer programmer on the mission, you won't have anything else to do with the computers right now, so you can help with setting up instruments.

Your destination is Tithonium Chasma, one part of the great Mariner Valley (Valles Marineris). The edge of the valley is about 300 miles (483 km) away, and it will take you about two days to get there. The commander will drive slowly and carefully on this first trip. The ride back will probably be faster.

The rover has large, flexible wheels, excellent for cushioning the passengers against the rocky surface. It is also quite big, almost like a camper you would use on Earth for vacation trips. Inside there are four beds and space for storing food, water, and air—even a small laboratory for doing important experiments on the site of a discovery. There are space-suit lockers for each crew member. An air lock is used to exit the rover so that breathable air can remain inside at all times. Normally, at least one member of the team will remain inside the rover to come to the assistance of anyone who is in trouble.

It is a nice clear day on Mars. The temperature outside is about -55° Fahrenheit (-48° Celsius). Not bad for a late summer morning. The high will be about -20° Fahrenheit (-29° Celsius), and tonight the temperature could fall to about -120° Fahrenheit (-84° Celsius).

You have become pretty good at getting into your suit. In just twenty minutes you are through the base camp air lock and strolling toward the rover. It is parked about 100 yards (91 m) from the base. Glancing around, you see many footprints in the loose red soil of Mars. The area around the base certainly has been explored in detail during this first week on Mars. The storage compartments on the lander are already filled with a large collection of Martian rocks, soil, and dust.

You also helped examine a strange ditch in the ground not far from where you landed. From orbit, you had been able to see that it was just one of five that crossed the surface here, looking like a scratch from a large five-fingered hand. The geologist thinks it has something to do with seismic activity. It may actually be a series of faults.

The commander welcomes you at the hatch of the rover. Over your suit radio she says, "All set? Got your toothbrush?"

Soon you are gliding along the Martian landscape, heading off to a new adventure. Along the way you encounter several small craters. The commander takes the rover up along the lip of one of them.

The view into the crater is spectacular. The crater is about two miles (3 km) across, and the bottom is about half a mile (.8 km) below the plain you are driving across. It looks different from the craters you have seen on the Moon. The Moon's craters were always very fresh looking, as if they had just been formed the day before. This crater on Mars looks old. The sides have collapsed in some areas, with big landslides spilling onto the floor of the crater. There are sand dunes piled up at the bottom. The lip of the crater itself is smooth and rounded, not sharp and pointed like many of the craters on the Moon.

As evening begins to fall, the commander brings the rover to a stop. "We've covered about 180 miles (290 km) today, so we're doing great," she tells you.

In the short time you've been on Mars, everyone has fallen in love with the sunset. This evening the sky becomes a deep fire-engine red; then after the sun sets, it slowly fades until the horizon seems to be glowing with a dull heat. Thin hazes become visible, a brighter and somewhat violet hue setting them apart from the surrounding sky.

As you crawl under the covers for some sleep that night, you notice slight sounds. The thin air doesn't carry sound very well, but now and then you notice the wind blowing outside. It seems just a little like Earth.

The next morning you're in the rover again. At an average speed of 30 miles (48 km) per hour it should only take about another four hours to reach the valley. The same scene of rocks and red dust continues to surround you. There is nothing to hint at the big change to come.

Just as your stomach tells you that it's lunchtime, the rover comes to a stop. You hear the commander exclaim, "Oh my!" Stepping into the cockpit you find you are suddenly unable to breathe. The scene outside the windows has you frozen in place.

Only a few feet in front of the rover the ground slopes suddenly downward. There, stretched out to the horizon is a vast valley. At the bottom of the valley are piles of rubble where great landslides have come to rest. Fields of huge sand dunes fill much of the floor. The walls show signs of layers, indicating changes that must have occurred on Mars in the distant past. The edge of the valley reaches as far as you can see.

A particularly loud growl from your stomach reminds you it's time to eat. Everyone excitedly eats a quick snack. Then it's into the space suits and out the air lock, ready to explore!

Walking to the edge of the slope you look downward. It must be a mile (1.6 km) or more to the valley floor. The slope starts out rather steeply, flattening out near the bottom. It would be impossible to walk down safely. You ask the geologist how stable the ground is here. Could it collapse into the valley like the landslides you can see down there? He tells you that is unlikely. Most of these landslides probably occurred millions of years ago as water was sucked out of the ground by the dry Martian climate.

The commander pulls out some rope from the front of the rover, attached to a large spool. "We've got about a quarter mile of this. Let's take a look at what's down there." She asks the biologist to stay behind for now, in case of any trouble.

The space suits make the climb rather difficult, even in the light gravity. About an hour later, you have all reached a small ledge. The color of the rock here is a bit darker. The geologist eagerly collects a sample. He also sets up a mini weather station. Then he collects some additional samples for the biologist, looking for any obvious signs of water or life in the rock. "Just one fossil," he says, "would sure make the climb back up seem a lot easier!"

After a short rest and a chance to enjoy the scenery, the group starts back up the face of the cliff. It takes longer, but finally you all return to the rover. The scientists immediately begin studying their samples. The commander radios the landing base, reporting that all is well and that you will start back tomorrow. You stretch back on your bunk, tired and a bit dazed. What an incredible world!

The next morning you arise a bit earlier than the others. The Sun is not yet quite over the horizon as you look toward the valley. The dark shadows make it difficult to see anything down in that deep hole. Then, as the first rays of sunlight begin to wash across the landscape, you see something wispy drift up out of the valley. It vanishes almost immediately. A few moments later, another slight wisp appears and fades away. The sunlight now begins to penetrate the very upper levels of the valley. Like little waves on an ocean, you see many faint wisps reach up out of the shadows and into the Sun and disappear. You run to the instrument console and check the readings on the weather station left down in the valley. "Hey, look at this!" you call out. The relative humidity reads 100 percent. Those are clouds drifting in the morning air. Water vapor! In the thin Martian air it doesn't take much water to saturate the air fully, but it sure is a lot more than you've seen before in this dry world.

The rising Sun quickly warms and evaporates the clouds. As you pull away and head back to base, the air in the valley is once again clear and dry.

THE GREAT THUNDER MOUNTAIN

Four days out from base camp you arrive at the foot of Ascraeus Mons. This is one of the giant volcanoes in the region of Mars called the Tharsis Ridge. It is the northernmost of a group of three volcanoes that sits east of the great Olympus Mons. The other two are Pavonis Mons and Arsia Mons. It is possible on a map to draw a straight line that just about perfectly connects the center of the mouths, or **caldera**, of these three volcanoes. Even farther to the north along the same line are several more somewhat smaller volcanoes.

You have traveled over 200 miles (322 km) across ancient lava flows. To reach the summit of Ascraeus Mons, you will have to go another 100 miles (161 km). The slope is quite gradual so the rover will be able to take you up.

Over the course of two more days, the ascent of Ascraeus Mons continues without problems. There are occasional deep ravines that must be driven around but nothing that completely blocks the way. The driver, the mission copilot, seems calm and confident as you climb nearly ten miles (16 km) into the sky.

The lava flows around you are different compared to the older ground near the landing site. There are almost no craters and very little sand or dust. The land is rather rugged, with lots of rocks and sharp-edged boulders. You are glad to have the seat belt as the ride gets rough. The higher you climb and the thinner the atmosphere becomes, the less erosion has taken place.

Finally, about 20 miles (32 km) from the actual caldera, the slope flattens out. You are now driving across a nearly level plain, littered

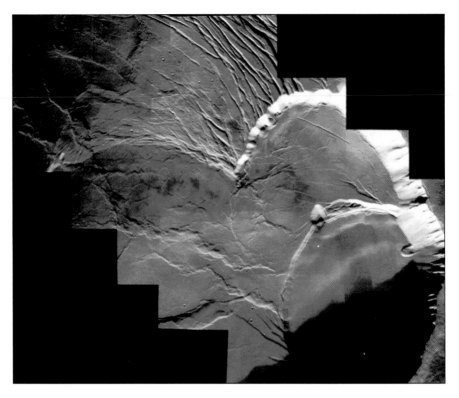

The floor of the giant caldera of Olympus Mons holds a record of ancient eruptions that may have helped shape the planet Mars.

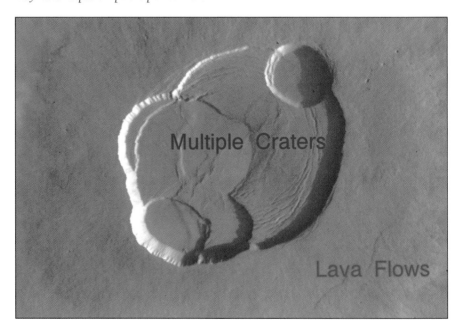

The multiringed caldera of Olympus Mons indicates repeated periods of activity and quiet.

with the rocky fragments ejected from the most recent eruptions of Ascraeus Mons.

Near sunset you reach the caldera. The Sun is directly in front of you as the rover pulls to a stop. Stretching nearly 40 miles (64 km) to the distant horizon is the deep throat of this massive volcano.

Long shadows create a sharp image of the huge depth of the caldera. The edge is a sheer cliff, dropping hundreds of feet to the floor below. Even in the dim evening light, you can still see the many levels to this volcanic crater. Each represents different eruptions. The central level is the only one forming a complete circle. It is also the deepest and the youngest. Surrounding it are partial circles—arcs—that formed the main caldera in other more distant ages. .

The mission geologist is very excited. Nowhere on Earth is there a volcano of this size! The geologist must be imagining a day long ago when the powerful forces of liquid rock surged out of the planet to form this monstrous mountain.

Looking toward the sunset you strain your eyes, looking for an even greater wonder. Somewhere, out there in the west, is Olympus Mons. Hundreds of miles away, the curvature of the planet is too great, even from this great height, to catch a glimpse of the 300-mile-wide (483 km) pile of ancient lava. It will await the arrival of future explorers.

As the light fades, you and your fellow explorers prepare for sleep. Tomorrow the caldera of Ascraeus Mons awaits you.

THE LONGEST ICE AGE

Six years have passed since the first expedition landed on Mars. As a meteorologist on the third Martian lander mission, you have the chance to see the north polar cap—a dream come true.

You landed at a location of about 73°N latitude, 193°W longitude, right next to the rather large crater Korolev. This seemed like a good location since the crater shielded a deposit of frost even during the height of the Martian summer. However, the frost layer was thin and rich in carbon dioxide, or dry ice, instead of water ice. Now the trip to the polar cap will be somewhat rushed. With summer beginning to come to a close, the polar region becomes more treacherous as the ice cap grows. Now is the time to go and recover as much water ice as possible. Supplying the base with water has become a major goal of the expedition. The science experiments have become less important.

After unpacking the rover from the cargo/fuel factory, the commander found that one of the wheels was damaged. That could have spelled the end of any long-distance exploration. Luckily, the crew was able to repair the wheel.

The edge of the permanent ice cap should be somewhere between 83° and 85°N latitude. That makes it a trip of between 350 to 400 miles (564 to 644 km). At 15 to 20 miles (24 to 32 km) per hour for five to eight hours per day, the trip will take four to five days.

In fact, the trip takes almost six days. To avoid two large cliffs, you must go more than 50 miles (81 km) out of the way each time. As you finally near the polar cap, frost becomes thicker and thicker, covering much of the surface. Even at high noon the temperature remains near

-70° Fahrenheit (-57° Celsius). Finally, a bright white cliff rears up in front of you. The cap!

In Alaska you had visited some of the glaciers pouring out of the mountains. Ice that had piled up for centuries slowly slid down mountainsides, finally crumbling and melting in the warm valleys. In Antarctica you had seen the vast ice sheets that covered the continent, thousands of feet thick. Within them, snow from prehistoric times carried information about climate and geologic changes on planet Earth that was available in no other place.

What can the polar caps tell about the past climate of Mars?

The rover comes to a stop, and soon you are into your suit and out of the air lock. You feel the frost crunch under your boots, like a fresh fall of dry snow on Earth.

The ice cliff face is about 40 feet (12 m) high. "One of the small ones," you comment. "There are some nearly 200 feet (61 m) tall farther north."

Much of the frost around you is made up of carbon dioxide. The goal, however, is to find water ice. Reaching the cliff face, you touch it with your glove. A coating of frost comes free and tumbles to the ground. You pull out your pick and begin chipping at the ice. You want to get a good chunk. Several minutes pass until a piece about one foot long and several inches thick comes free. You quickly grab it before it can crash to the ground.

The south pole of Mars seems to be mostly frozen carbon dioxide, also known as dry ice.

You turn the chunk of ice over in your hands. It is cloudy and pinkish in color. Dust and dirt are trapped within, prisoners from some dust storm of long ago.

"Help!" The call comes across your radio. Dropping the ice chunk into the pouch by your side, you look around. The commander is slightly crouched over, looking down into some kind of hole in the ground.

You run over to see what's happening. The ground is a bit slippery here, even in spiked boots. Down below in a trench is the mission geologist, down on all fours, his hands clutching a ledge of ice. The ground beneath him is slanted downward into the deep trench. If he loses his grip, he will slide beyond sight, into a dark gap in the frozen ground.

"We've got to get him out of there fast!" the commander says.

"I'm coming," calls the flight engineer. "I've got the rope."

Soon the rope is lowered to the geologist. He is strangely quiet and, at first, seems not to want to grab the rope. Then suddenly his hands slash across the ice surface. As he begins sliding downward, his hands grab at the rope. The ice ledge he had been holding onto now crumbles into tiny bits and pieces. For a moment it seems he has missed the rope, but then the rope grows taut as the full weight of the geologist becomes suspended from its end. Quickly you help pull him to safety.

"I could tell that piece of ice I was holding was very fragile. I was afraid to move or say anything," the geologist says later from the safety of the rover.

Still wearing thick gloves for protection, you have just pulled out the ice chunk you recovered from your suit pouch. It is quite frozen despite the warm temperature of the rover. Carbon dioxide ice will melt rapidly in these temperatures. This seems to be holding together pretty well. There is very little steam rising from the ice. Dry ice usually produces lots of steam. Cautiously you raise the ice to your nose. Carbon dioxide, though odorless, will make you cough if you breathe it in very much. You sniff deeply but find no discomfort.

The surface of the ice begins to take on a shiny coating. Slowly, a drop of liquid forms at the bottom and drops to the floor. Carbon dioxide, as it melts, becomes a gas, not a liquid. Yes, this is water ice! There's plenty of water here, enough to keep your base camp well supplied during the five hundred days you will spend on Mars.

CITY IN THE SAND

For twenty-three years spacecraft with astronaut crews have come to Mars. There are now two permanent bases. One is near the first landing site at 4°N latitude, 91°W longitude. From here expeditions to the Tharsis Ridge volcanoes and the deep canyons of the Valles Marineris complex are launched.

You have recently arrived to help establish the second permanent base, at 22°N latitude, 48°W longitude. This is a very important location. Just a few miles from here is the *Viking 1* lander, which has been on Mars for more than fifty years. Just the other day, the entire camp walked over to the lander. It was sitting in a pile of drifted dust, the footpads completely covered. The site is to be left as undisturbed as possible. A small plaque was attached to one leg. It read "Dedicated to the memory of Tim Mutch, whose imagination, verve, and resolve contributed greatly to the exploration of the solar system." Tim Mutch died before you were born, but he was one of the few who realized the value of space travel during a time when it wasn't very popular. Without him, the dream to explore Mars may have died long ago.

At the bottom of the plaque was a line marked "Emplaced." As commander of the mission, you had the responsibility of etching in the date: August 19, 2037.

With the camp established, it is time for exploration. Your first mission is a long one. You are to travel over 1,000 miles (1,610 km) to the northeast, to a place just east of the Acidalia Planitia. This location, at about 40°N and 9°W, has been a mystery ever since it was first seen by the Viking orbiters so many years ago.

Most of this trip is very uneventful, in fact, almost boring. The landscape is just flat, rocky plain. A few places appear to have been flooded long ago, and a crater is visible every now and then. For almost two weeks, you trek across this barren wilderness. You wish there were some faster means of getting around. Maybe the next mission will bring along one of the airplanes being developed on Earth for use on Mars. That would make a trip like this a lot easier.

Finally you approach your destination. This area has been photographed often from orbit. Each picture has raised the mystery to higher levels. This first visit should solve the puzzle.

Winding among some mountains, your rover suddenly comes upon a strange sight. A different mountain appears here but with a familiar shape. Though uneven and pitted by blowing sand and dust, there is no doubt that this mountain has the general form of a pyramid. Could it have formed naturally? Many scientists throughout the years have said this is the result of sand and dust carried by the wind sculpting the mountains into this form. They could be right. The pyramid seems very worn and hardly the perfect shape of the pyramids on Earth.

You leave the rover and walk up to touch the mountain. The surface is covered with loose sand and dust, that crumble in your hand and fall to the ground. You gaze up along one side, to a height of several hundred feet. You are not sure—it could be natural or maybe it's just very old. If people built it, who could they have been? Martians?

Continuing across the landscape, you see other strange mountains with vaguely pyramidal shapes. It is sort of eerie.

Suddenly you stop the rover. Before you is the strangest sight of all. Nearly a mile across, a low mound sits upon the sand. Silhouetted against the pink sky, you can see the outline of a face looking directly skyward, just as the famous pictures had shown.

Leaving the rover again, you and the rest of your companions approach this amazing feature. Drifts of sand rest at its base. You wade into the sand, your feet sinking nearly to your knees. You reach the wall of the mound and wipe your glove across the surface.

The sand falls away. For a moment you forget to breathe. Though it must be very old, there is no longer any doubt that this is not a feature formed by wind and sand. At some time intelligent beings lived here on this plain and left behind this monument and probably the pyramid mountains as well. You know because the surface of this mound is not one of simple stone. There are lines here, long horizontal ones and short vertical ones forming a familiar pattern. Bricks!

Were the builders native to Mars? Were they simply visitors, possibly from some distant star, in search of a new home? You look around at the sandy ground. Might the remains of their homes be buried here? Might skeletons of their dead be found, having waited for unknown thousands of years in this red soil to greet new explorers into space?

You have just become part of the greatest discovery in the history of humankind. What will it mean to the billions of other people back home to know that we are not alone in the universe?

EPILOGUE

MILLIONS OF BYTES TO MARS

I hope you have found this book an interesting introduction to the future exploration of Mars. These last four chapters were included to let you experience a small part of what it will be like when the big day arrives. Are you excited about Mars?

It may seem hard to have to wait, maybe twenty years or more, before the first landing on Mars. Would you like to start exploring Mars today? There are several ways you can do that.

This book, and others like it, are one way. Visit your library and look for other books on Mars. You might want to check out books about the various planets of the solar system too. There are many worlds to explore here in our solar system. You can compare them to what you have learned about Mars. It won't take long before you become a solar system expert!

There are also some good magazines you can read. *Sky and Telescope* and *Astronomy* magazines are two examples. Your library may carry these, and they can also be found at many bookstores and newsstands.

Is there a planetarium in your city? Sometimes if the local museum doesn't have a planetarium, you can find one at a nearby college. Planetariums often have shows for the public. Call the planetarium in your area. It may have a show about Mars or be planning to present one in the future. Let them know what you would like to see.

If you have a computer at home or at school, there is another way you can explore Mars. You need a CD-ROM drive for the computer. A CD-ROM drive uses disks just like the CDs that are used to play music.

Instead of music, however, data are stored on these disks. There are many disks available with information about space.

NASA has a collection of disks on Mars called *Mission to Mars: Digital Image Map*. It is a set of six CD-ROM disks containing about four gigabytes (4,000,000,000 bytes) of information in the form of images of Mars. Software is included on the disks for viewing the images on several types of computers, including Apple, Macintosh, and IBM compatibles. I used this set to explore Mars in preparation for writing this book. I also used it to help me create some of the pictures that I have included. For information or to order the disks, write to:

National Space Science Data Center
World Data Center-A for Rockets and Satellites
Code 633
Goddard Space Flight Center
Greenbelt, Maryland 20771

Tell your friends and family about Mars. Write a special report about Mars for your class at school. Most of all, keep learning about Mars and about all kinds of science and math. Then you will be ready when your chance comes to travel *Millions of Miles to Mars*!

Joseph W. Kelch

GLOSSARY

acceleration—an increase in speed over time.

aerobraking—the slowing down of a spacecraft as it enters a planet's atmosphere.

air—the mixture of invisible, odorless gases (nitrogen, oxygen, and others) that surrounds Earth.

caldera—mouth of a volcano, where eruptions have occurred.

carbon dioxide—heavy, colorless gas (CO_2) that does not support combustion, dissolves in water to form carbonic acid, is formed especially in animal respiration (humans exhale carbon dioxide) and in the decay or combustion of animal and vegetable matter, and is absorbed in the air by plants in photosynthesis.

continental drift—slow movement of the continents, which are floating on plates that are pushed about by the molten rock beneath Earth's crust.

ellipse—an oval, such as the orbits of all the planets and moons in the solar system.

energy—something that all matter can be converted into.

fixed stars—the background of stars visible from Earth, that appear as recognized patterns called constellations.

friction—rubbing of one body or object against another; resistance to relative motion between two bodies or objects in contact.

fusion—the combination of two or more atoms to form one larger atom of another element, also producing a large amount of energy.

gravity—the gravitation attraction of the mass of Earth, the Moon, or a planet for bodies at or near its surface.

inertia—a property of matter by which it remains at rest or in uniform motion in the same straight line unless acted upon by some external (outside) force.

ions—electrically charged atoms.

launch windows—the times that are best for launching a spaceship, requiring the least amount of fuel and time to reach a destination.

Life Zone—the region that is neither too near nor too far from the Sun to allow life, with the right balance of light and heat, as on Earth.

matter—the substance of all things in the universe.

opposition—when a planet farther from the Sun than Earth is directly opposite the Sun in our sky and closest to Earth.

oxygen—an element found free as a colorless, tasteless, odorless gas in Earth's atmosphere. Oxygen forms about 21 percent of Earth's atmosphere. Also found combined with hydrogen to form water in rocks, minerals, and in numerous organic compounds.

photosynthesis—a chemical process by which a green plant makes use of the sun's energy in the form of light, converts the carbon dioxide in the air into sugar, and gives off oxygen as a waste product.

planetarium—theater where the night sky is simulated by using special projectors.

refractor—type of telescope that uses lenses rather than mirrors to focus the light.

retrograde loop—seemingly backward motion of Mars (or other planets farther from the Sun than Earth) against the background of the stars as Earth passes Mars once every 780 days while orbiting the Sun.

solar system—the planets, moons, asteroids, and comets that orbit the Sun.

Space Age—beginning with the launch of *Sputnik 1* in 1957, the commitment by both the United States and the former Soviet Union to explore space.

terraforming—process of changing a world to make it more Earth-like.

transfer orbit—the path a spaceship follows to move from an orbit around one world to another.

FURTHER READING

Mars and space exploration have long been popular topics of both science fact and fiction. You should have no trouble finding many interesting books to read. Here are a few suggestions organized by category.

Fiction

Berna, Paul. *Continent in the Sky*. New York: Abelard-Schuman, 1963.

_____. *Threshold of the Stars*. New York: Abelard-Schuman, 1960.

Bova, Ben. *Mars*. New York: Bantam Books, 1992.

Bradbury, Ray. *The Martian Chronicles*. Garden City, NY: Doubleday, 1950.

Burroughs, Edgar Rice. *A Fighting Man of Mars*. New York: Ballantine Books, 1981.

_____. *Llana of Gathol and John Carter of Mars*. Garden City, NY: Doubleday, 1977.

_____. *A Princess of Mars*. Garden City, NY: Doubleday, 1970.

_____. *Three Martian Novels: Thuvia, Maid of Mars, The Chessmen of Mars*, and *The Mastermind of Mars*. New York: Dover Publications, 1962.

Robinson, Kim Stanley. *Green Mars*. New York: Bantam Books, 1994.

_____. *Red Mars*. New York: Bantam Books, 1993.

Wells, H. G. *The War of the Worlds*. New York: Platt & Munk, 1963.

Nonfiction

Batson, Raymond M. *Atlas of Mars*. Washington, D.C.: Scientific and Technical Information Branch, NASA. Published by the U.S. Government Printing Office, 1979.

Berger, Melvin. *Discovering Mars: The Amazing Story of the Red Planet*. New York: Scholastic, 1992.

_____. *If You Lived on Mars*. New York: Lodestar Books, 1988.

Brewer, Duncan. *Mars*. New York: Cavendish, 1990.

Carlotto, Mark J. *The Martian Enigmas*. Berkeley, CA: North Atlantic Books, 1991.

Cattermole, Peter John. *Mars*. New York: Facts-on-File, 1989.

Cooper, Henry S. F., Jr. *The Search for Life on Mars*. New York: Holt, Rinehart and Winston, 1980.

Corrick, James A. *Mars*. New York: Franklin Watts, 1991.

DeSomma, Vincent V. *The Mission to Mars and Beyond*. New York: Chelsea House, 1992.

Evans, Barry. *The Wrong-Way Comet and Other Mysteries of Our Solar System*. Blue Ridge Summit, PA: Tab Books, 1992.

Fisher, David E. *The Third Experiment: Is There Life on Mars?* New York: Atheneum, 1985.

Hoyt, William Graves. *Lowell and Mars*. Tucson: University of Arizona Press, 1976.

Oberg, James E. *Mission to Mars: Plans and Concepts for the First Manned Landing*. Harrisburg, PA: Stackpole Books, 1982.

Powers, Robert M. *Mars: Our Future on the Red Planet*. Boston: Houghton Mifflin, 1986.

Pozos, Randolfo Rafael. *The Face on Mars*. Chicago: Chicago Review Press, 1986.

Vogt, Gregory. *Viking and the Mars Landing*. Brookfield, CT: Millbrook Press, 1991.

Walter, William J. *Space Age*. New York: Random House, 1992.

Wilford, John Noble. *Mars Beckons*. New York: Knopf, 1990.

Recordings

The War of the Worlds. The actual radio broadcast by the Mercury Theatre on the Air as heard October 30, 1938. Distributed by Evolution 4001.

Videocassettes

Mars: The Red Planet. Pictures of the red planet's surface sent by Viking and Mariner satellites. 30 minutes. VHS format. Distributed by Videotakes.

On Robot Wings: A Flight Through the Solar System. VHS format. Whittier, CA: Finley-Holiday Film Corporation, 1992.

Planet Mars and Mercury. Imaginative theories about Mars are traced. Includes color pictures of the planet's surface plus animation of how geological features evolved. 52 minutes. VHS format. Whittier, CA: Finley-Holiday Film Corporation.

CD-ROM Computer Software Products

Mars Explorer, Virtual Reality Laboratories, Inc., 2341 Ganador Court, San Luis Obispo, CA 93401 (1-800-829-8754).

NASA Viking images seamlessly tied together to allow exploration of Mars. Animation of the rotation of Mars. Images can be used with other applications. Overlay of names for features available. For IBM PCs.

Redshift: The Multimedia Planetarium, Maris Multimedia, Ltd. (1-800-336-0185).

Besides exploring Mars, this disk will show you the motion of the planets, views of the night sky from any location, hundreds of astrophotos, and the *Penguin Dictionary of Astronomy*. Macintosh and IBM PC Windows.

Vista Pro CD-ROM, Virtual Reality Laboratories, Inc., 2341 Ganador Court, San Luis Obispo, CA 93401 (1-800-829-8754).

Image data from Mars used to produce highly detailed views of the surface of Mars. Earth data also included. Create your own animation files. You can add trees, lakes, rivers, and buildings to create a more

Earth-like Mars. You can even "fly" across the surface. Create stereo image pairs for 3-D effects. Outputs to many graphic formats for use in other graphic applications. IBM PC DOS version now available. Coming soon for Macintosh. Amiga version available on floppy disk.

INDEX

italic page numbers indicate illustration

MAP OF MARS

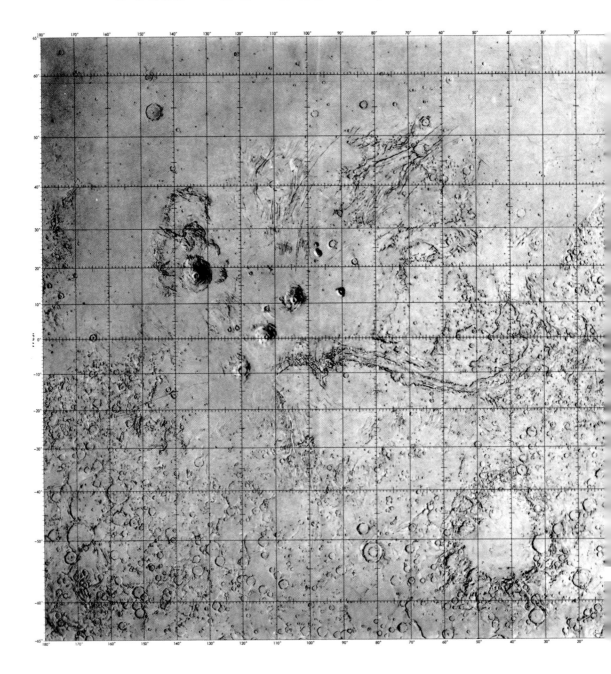

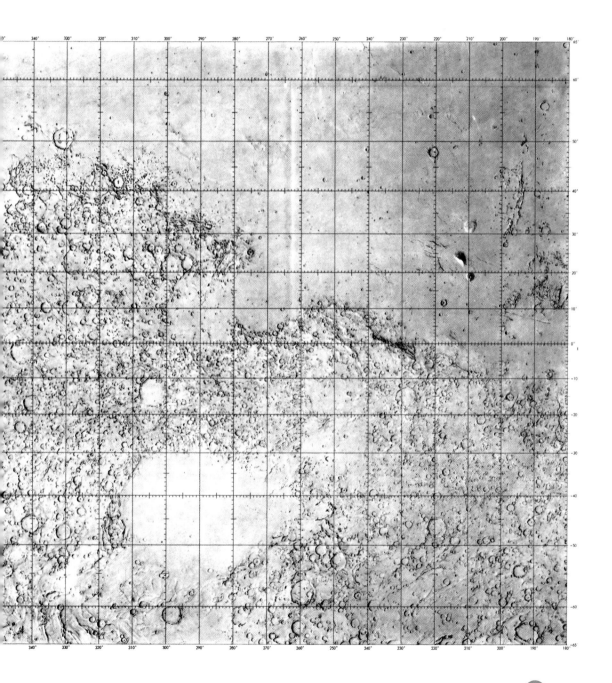